CHEESE MAKING AT HOME

Cheese Making at Home:

The Complete Illustrated Guide

BY DON RADKE

DOUBLEDAY & COMPANY, INC.

GARDEN CITY, NEW YORK

1974

Library of Congress Cataloging in Publication Data
Radke, Don, 1940–
    Cheese making at home.

    1. Cheese.   2. Cookery (Cheese)   I. Title.
SF271.R28   641.6′7′3
ISBN 0-385-01887-8
Library of Congress Catalog Card Number 74–1505

To my entire family,
who have to live with me.

CONTENTS

viii   *Contents*

INTRODUCTION

"How my life was changed by a cheese kit" could well be the title for this book, since it was the advent of the cheese kit that prompted me to make my own cheese. At first the problems seemed insurmountable. There were simply no procedures available to the general public telling one how to make cheese. The kit instructions provided a starting point but more information and variety were needed.

My research began about seven miles from my home at a local cheese factory. From the kind people there I learned the procedures for several varieties of cheese and the address of the local dairy laboratory. The Department of Agriculture at the University of Wisconsin gave me considerable information about cheese making also. Now my problem was not how to do it, but how to do it at home. The information I had been able to obtain was invariably for two thousand pounds of milk or more; as much as twenty thousand pounds of milk is processed in a single vat in a cheese factory. I wanted to make cheese in a kettle on my electric range and it was the procedure for doing this that required considerable time and experimentation. The refrigerator began to fill with unpalatable lumps of plastic milk; anything good was consumed immediately.

It was about this time that it came to my attention that there were many people who were trying to do the same thing. Making all sorts of cheeses at home was not such a strange hobby after all. Unfortunately for most home cheese makers, many parts of the country have poorly developed dairy industries and the information that I had obtained was not available to them. And so, it is for those people and the people who believe that homemade is still the best, and for anyone else who likes doing things for himself, that I have compiled the material in this book.

1

A SHORT HISTORY OF
CHEESE MAKING

Cheese—the food of the gods—has been a staple commodity for thousands of years. In fact, since man first learned to communicate by scratching pictures on the walls of his cave, milk, butter, and cheese have been on the menu. The whole dairy industry, after milking the cow, is probably based on a prehistoric accident.

Picture a noble primate setting out for a day of hunting. It's July and it's hot, so our distant relative packs a lunch of buffalo milk in a handy gourd, slings it over his shoulder, and sets off. Six hours later, hot, tired, and hungry he sits down to enjoy his lunch. He takes a drink from his gourd and finds the contents slightly sour but not unpleasant. He also discovers that the inside of the gourd is coated with a sweet grease. Being a clever fellow, he soon learns that although milk sours quickly the sweet grease can be kept around for days. And so butter comes upon the scene.

Our friendly native is even luckier with his next adventure.

Once again it is time to set out on a much-needed hunting trip. Looking around the cave, he finds that every gourd is full of churned milk: the wife and kids having been jogging all over the neighborhood the day before. But, being a resourceful person, he decides to carry his milk in the caveman's answer to the plastic bottle, a goat's stomach. So, once again, he sets off with his milk sloshing over his shoulder. At noon he decides to have his lunch of buttermilk and butter. As soon as he starts drinking he knows that something has gone wrong for the milk is not sour, it is sweet. There is also no grease stuck to the inside of the stomach, but rather a gelatinous mass in the bottom. Curds and whey have replaced the milk with the help of the enzyme present in the stomach and cheese has been born.

Records from Egypt show detailed accounts of butter and cheese making from 4000 B.C. onward. The Vedic hymns of India suggest using the milk and butter from cattle rather than killing the cow for the meat, which was considered a sin. Cheese is also mentioned in the Bible. David carried ten cheeses to the army before going off to slay Goliath and the athletic stadium of Jerusalem was in the valley known as *Tyropaeon* (the valley of the cheese makers).

Cheese was included in the offerings to the gods on Mount Olympus. Homer, Hippocrates, and Aristotle all mention cheese in their writings. Roving herdsmen, in their search for green pastures, spread the art of cheese making throughout Europe. During the height of the Roman Empire cheese making became an important industry. Cheese became so highly esteemed that the ancient Romans would compare a much-sought-after lady to a good cheese. A comparison which, I dare say, would earn a cold bed today.

The economic values in cheese making were not ignored either. It didn't take long for people to learn that cheese making was a convenient way of converting perishable milk into an easily preserved, nutritious, palatable, and digestible product. It was also noted that a wagonload of cheese sold for considerably more than a wagonload of milk and that the cheese could wait around for a good price. No self-respecting entrepreneur could turn down a business that promising, so cheese making flourished everywhere.

Many modern cheeses can be traced back for centuries. The records of the Monastery of Conques in France mention Roquefort for the first time in A.D. 1070 and as with many inventions, it was discovered by accident. Cheddar has been known for over five hundred years. Napoleon named Camembert cheese when he discovered that it had no name, and the Bishop of Milan made a gift of Gorgonzola to the school of St. Ambrosia in A.D. 879. An early variety of Parmesan used the moon as its trademark and was probably the first connection between the moon and cheese, green or otherwise.

Cheese making was, however, a family craft handed down through the generations. It has only been in recent years that antiseptic standardization has taken the family art out of cheese making and made it a factory product. Now that people are getting back to nature, cheese making can once again become an individual craft in which a person can express his talents. And that, in short, is what this book is all about.

2

THE CHEESE-MAKING PROCESS

A TECHNICAL DESCRIPTION

There seems to be a trend in writing in this country which dictates that a deep scientific explanation be given for every simple process. Cheese making is a rather simple process, so, naturally, I feel obligated to give a technical description of cheese making for the benefit of the people who like tossing around long Latin names and four-syllable words.

The technical section is limited to the first pages of this chapter and can safely be omitted by anyone without a taste for *Streptococcus lactis*. The second part of this chapter is important and should not be overlooked. Now, for those of you who have not skipped ahead to the Materials and General Procedure section, here is the scientific explanation.

Cheese is made by the controlled syneresis of the rennet-milk coagulum, and the removal of whey by acid development, heat, and cutting of the curd. Lactic acid organisms, primarily *Streptococcus lactis* and *Streptococcus cremoris,* are added to milk as a lactic starter to produce acid and lower the pH from 6.6 to about 5. The milk is warmed to provide for proper growth of the organisms and hence, acid development. Cutting the curd increases the effective surface area in the coagulum and accelerates syneresis.

Acid development, then, is critical to the entire cheese-making process. Failure to develop acid properly can result in a soft, mushy curd and undesirable bacteria growth. The increase of titratable acid dictates when rennet is to be added. Too much acid and the curd will not release its whey for several days. Too little acid and the apparently dry cheese will begin leaking whey several weeks after pressing.

Rennet, a proteolytic enzyme, is added to clot the milk. Rennet is preferred to other enzymes because of its high clotting power over its proteolytic power. Overactive proteolysis can produce bad flavors, bitterness, and premature release of whey from the curd, allowing undesirable bacteria growth. Rennet acts on the caseins of milk by first acting on the protein to break down its protective barriers and then to precipitate them as a coagulum.

In cheese making 95 percent of the water held in the milk is released. This is accomplished through the combined effects of heat, acid, rennet, and the breaking up of the rennet-formed curd. Heat must be applied at a rate sufficiently slow to allow moisture to escape from the center of each curd particle. Excess heat causes a case hardening effect of the curd trapping whey in the inner section of the curd. As moisture is exuded by the curd, it draws together into a mass of granules.

During cooking, the acid concentration has continued to rise to the point where the whey must be drawn off or the curd will become too firm for proper matting and will produce a crumbly structure. Draining the whey at the right moment is critical to successful cheese making. After draining, the curd is salted and put to press in order to give the cheese a shape and compact the curd into a cohesive unit.

After removal from the press the cheese is allowed to ripen. During ripening, proteolysis of the curd is the major chemical change. This slow digestion of the protein is what converts the rubbery curd of fresh cheese to the mellow and waxy product of ripened cheese. Some breakdown of fats also occurs during the ripening time and lactose is fermented to produce lactic acid, acetic acid, propionic acid, and carbon dioxide.

This technical presentation is far from complete and the processes vary with the type of cheese being produced, but it should give the reader some idea of the complex physical and chemical reactions taking place when cheese is being made.

MATERIALS AND GENERAL PROCEDURES

The USDA recognizes eighteen distinct varieties of cheese and this book will give the procedures to make fourteen of them plus several variations. The varieties with which we will concern ourselves are brick, Camembert, Cheddar, Edam, Gouda, Swiss, cream, cottage, Neufchâtel, Parmesan, Cacio-cavallo, Romano, Blue, and Whey cheese. Some of these will be almost impossible to make at home because controlled humidity, aging rooms, and special mold growths are not available for home use; however, I will discuss them and the possibilities of making them in your home. I will start with the cheeses easiest to make and progress, as nearly as possible, to the very difficult. I would strongly suggest making all of the cheeses detailed in Chapter Three before attempting anything more difficult. The cottage and cream cheeses can tolerate an inexperienced cheese maker more than most other varieties.

At this point, I am about to make a few assumptions.

1. You like to eat cheese,
2. You like to mess around in the kitchen,
3. You have some spare time, and
4. You like to show off your incredible genius.

The above being correctly assumed, I will now proceed, in very general terms, with making cheese at home.

Every variety of cheese known has certain characteristics in common. First, they are all made from the milk of certain mammals; most commonly cow, goat, and sheep. Other mammals whose milk can be used are horses, buffalo, and reindeer. There are some types of milk which will not clot with rennet, so don't run out to get gorilla milk if you can't tolerate an unsuccessful project.

Secondly, all cheese starts by souring the milk. Pure, unpasteurized, unfortified, unhomogenized, unirradiated, unsterilized milk will sour quickly by letting it stand at room temperature. However, since most of us do not have our own cow, we will have to be content with a gallon or two of what's available from the supermarket. I would, however, recommend pasteurized milk regardless of where it comes from. To sour milk from the store it is necessary to use a lactic starter. The starter which we will use is *cultured* buttermilk. About one half of the buttermilk sold commercially is active and, therefore, suitable for use as a starter. *Cultured* buttermilk means that the buttermilk was made by growing acid-producing organisms in milk. Dry, powdered buttermilk and buttermilk-flavored milk will not work as a starter because it does not contain the necessary living organisms. The starter should be as fresh as possible, never more than about ten days old. If there is any doubt concerning the activity of the starter, perform this simple test. Place four ounces of warm milk into a clean glass and stir in two teaspoons of buttermilk. Set the glass in a warm place for twenty-four hours. If after twenty-four hours you still have a glass of warm *liquid* milk, you do not have an active starter. The starter is all right to use if the milk has become firm and gelatinous; it should have the consistency of pudding and a good flavor, similar to sour cream.

Thirdly, the milk is clotted or coagulated. This is done, in some cases, by adding rennet and in others by letting the milk coagulate of its own accord. Most cheeses, however, are clotted by rennet. Rennet is an enzyme extracted from the fourth or true stomach of a calf. Rennet is a powerful enzyme and is capable of both clotting the protein in milk and digesting it. It is particularly useful in cheese making because its clotting power is much greater than its digestive power. Excessive digestion of the milk protein can cause serious defects in the finished cheese.

Fourthly, the coagulated milk is cut or broken up to release the whey and form curds. The curds are the individual nodules of semi-solidified milk casein which will eventually be pressed into a finished cheese. The whey is the clear liquid remaining. The coagulated milk, before cutting, is like a single, gigantic curd. Cutting this single unit into many small cubes breaks an invisible seal and allows the whey to escape from each cube. As the whey runs out, the cubes shrink in size and become firm; as the cubes shrink they form nodules called curds. Cooking accelerates the removal of whey from the curd and helps it to become firm.

Fifthly, the curd is consolidated or matted. This is accomplished by placing the curd into a press and compacting it into a solid unit. The pressure needed to do this varies from nearly nothing in making Neufchâtel to several tons for Cheddar. Cottage cheese is not pressed at all and is consumed as loose curds.

Sixthly, the fresh or green cheese is allowed to ripen. Some cheese, like certain wines, deteriorate with ripening and must be consumed as soon as possible; cottage cheese, for example. Other types, such as Parmesan and Cheddar, are not at their peak until nearly a year has passed.

The above procedure will produce cheese of one kind or another. To produce a particular kind of cheese, certain other factors must be considered. The most important of these factors are:

1. the type of milk,
2. how long it sours,
3. the use of rennet,
4. the renneting temperature, the cooking temperature, and the cooking time,
5. how fine the curd is cut,
6. how firm the curd is pressed,
7. and the time, temperature, and humidity during ripening.

In general, the hardness of a cheese is controlled by the extent to which the whey is drawn from the curd. The more acid developed, the higher the cooking temperature, the finer the curd is cut and the longer the length of time over which these all happen, the drier will be the resulting cheese. With all this in mind, we can proceed to gather some tools.

The quantity of milk with which we will work will usually be one gallon. This is a convenient amount in that it is easy to handle, cooking utensils are readily available, the kettle fits nicely on a modern range and if disaster occurs, there is not too much to throw out. Some types of cheese, however, will be made with as much as ten gallons of milk because of curing problems encountered with very small quantities of cheese.

The first and most important utensil is a good kettle that can hold a gallon of milk with some room left over for stirring. Obtain a second kettle large enough to put the cooking kettle inside; in this way a water bath can be used to heat the milk and curd, and the temperature is more uniform and easily controlled. A wire cooking rack placed in the bottom of the larger kettle will provide for water circulation and will prevent water from being trapped under the cooking kettle and becoming superheated. I will refer to this double kettle arrangement as a "cheese cooking assembly."

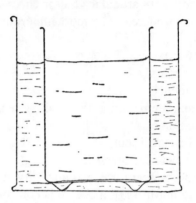

Figure 1. The kettle within a kettle "cheese cooking assembly." The inner kettle contains the coagulated milk and the outer kettle is filled with water to the same level as the milk. Note the wire rack under the smaller kettle.

The second item needed is an accurate thermometer designed for liquids that reads up to about 150 degrees. (All of the temperatures used in this book are in degrees Fahrenheit.) A photography or chemical supply shop is a good source for this. A good buy is a thermometer incorporated in a stirring paddle such as a ham boiling thermometer.

In addition, you will need a long knife or spatula to cut the curd, a package of cheesecloth, a colander (about a one-gallon size), cheese coloring, and rennet tablets.

Color tablets and rennet tablets compounded for one gallon of milk are available by mail from Wagner Products Division, Hustisford, Wisconsin 53034. If you plan to make cheese in any kind of quantity, however, it might be to your advantage to obtain rennet and coloring materials from a commercial distributor (see Appendix 1).

Cheese coloring is added to the ripening milk only to add aesthetic appeal to the cheese. The coloring material is extract of annatto. This extract is obtained from the fruit of the annatto tree which is common in many tropical climates. For cheese making, the extract is mixed with alkaline compounds to ensure even coloring of all the milk solids and fat. An oily compound of annatto is used to color butter and will not work with cheese. Alkaline annatto is universally recognized as the best coloring agent for cheese and recent tests have shown it to be non-carcinogenic. So why, you may ask, bother to color cheese anyway? Answer: to make it look pretty.

It will also be necessary to construct a cheese press. First, obtain a metal or plastic sleeve about the size of a one-pound coffee can (four inches in diameter and six inches long). This sleeve should be straight sided with no ribs or impressions. Cut two discs the same diameter as the inside of the sleeve and drill eight three-sixteenths-inch holes in a random pattern. Also, drill a five-sixteenths-inch hole in the center of each disc.

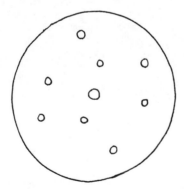

Figure 2. The cheese pressing disc.

The discs can be made from metal, plastic or plexiglas, or even hardwood. Be certain that the material is thick enough so that it will not bend when pressing the cheese. Hobby stores have small pieces of very hard one-eighth-inch plywood which would be excellent; the plywood must be an exterior grade. Purchase a one-quarter-inch threaded rod, zinc or nickel plated if you can find one, and two, one-quarter-inch wing nuts. The rod should be cut to the same length as the sleeve.

All the utensils should be carefully washed before using and rinsed with boiling water. Do not pour boiling water on your thermometer because this will ruin it. Keep the thermometer out of the automatic dishwasher, also. The cheesecloth should be boiled for five minutes before using. Doing this will help to prevent undesirable bacteria and mold growth.

Many of these items can be obtained by purchasing one of the cheese-making kits currently on the market, in particular, the cheese press and tablets.

Now that we have all of our tools and have cleared everyone out of the kitchen, let's make cheese.

3

COTTAGE AND CREAM CHEESE

Cottage cheese is a soft unripened cheese made from skimmed milk. It is high in protein, easily digested and remarkably low in calories.

SMALL CURD COTTAGE CHEESE

We will start with cottage cheese for several good reasons. First, it's easy; second, it is almost foolproof; and thirdly, it is better than anything you can buy at the store. Three really great reasons, in my opinion.

Natural small curd cottage cheese is made without rennet and has a high acid content giving it a delicious tartness. Most commercial grades of cottage cheese use rennet to speed up the manufacturing process; the use of rennet, however, reduces the acid content and in effect produces large curd cottage cheese.

For cottage cheese you will need one gallon of fresh *skimmed* milk (pasteurized) and one-quarter cup of fresh cultured buttermilk. Put your "cheese cooking assembly" together and pour the skimmed milk into the inner (cooking) kettle. Now add warm water to the outside kettle until the water level is the same as the level of the milk. Gently heat the water until the milk is 72° (use your thermometer). When the milk is at the proper temperature, stir in the buttermilk. Set the kettle in a place which will stay at 72 to 80 degrees. Place a cover on the kettle to keep dirt and the cat out of the milk and you are done—for today.

What we have done is started skim milk to ripen. The buttermilk acts as the acid forming starter, and the process now requires only time to cause the milk to coagulate. Once the process has begun, do not disturb it, do not stir the milk, or even move the kettle. In fact, don't do anything to it for the next sixteen hours.

Sixteen hours after adding the starter the milk should be tested for coagulation. To do this, insert a clean knife into the curd at the side of the kettle. Using the flat side of the knife, gently pull the curd toward the center of the kettle. If the curd breaks smoothly away from the kettle sides, it is ready to cut.

This first test should find the milk still in a liquid condition. If the milk is coagulated after sixteen hours, use a little less starter for any future batches. If the milk has not coagulated yet, leave it stand undisturbed for another eight hours and test again. If the milk still has not coagulated, use more starter for future batches. Ideally, the curd should be ready for cutting twenty hours after adding the starter.

Regardless of how long it takes for this first batch to coagulate, it is acceptable for making into cottage cheese. If the milk hasn't coagulated after forty-eight hours, however, I would suspect an inactive starter. There is nothing to do with an inactive starter but to throw it out or drink it if you like buttermilk. The milk which has been sitting out for two days should be discarded. (Refer to Chapter 2 for a procedure to test starter activity.)

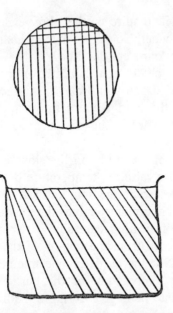

Figure 3. Make uniform vertical slices through the curd as in A, then turn the kettle and repeat the process making cuts perpendicular to the first cuts. Cut the curd at an angle starting with the shortest cut as in B, then turn the kettle and repeat the angled cuts.

The next step is to cut the curd into one-quarter-inch cubes. Insert a knife through the curd to the bottom of the kettle at the far side of the kettle. Pull the knife through the curd to the near side of the container. Remove the knife and repeat the process every one-quarter inch across the kettle. Turn the kettle a quarter turn and repeat the process.

Turn the kettle back to its original position and repeat the cutting, this time holding the knife at a 45-degree angle. Try to follow the original cutting lines. Again turn the kettle a quarter turn and repeat the cutting at a 45-degree angle. The same cutting procedure is followed wherever the curd is cut.

Some varieties will require cutting three-eighths, one-half or five-eighths-inch cubes. To do this, simply change the width of cut in each of the four steps described.

As you made each cut you should have noticed a clear liquid appearing the instant you broke the surface. This is whey. Cutting through the curd releases the whey and allows the cubes to contract. After cutting the curd, allow it to stand for ten minutes.

Place the cooking assembly on the stove and start heating the water slowly to raise the temperature of the curd to 100 degrees. Use the low or medium-low setting on an electric range. Place your thermometer into the curds and whey, and watch the rate of heating carefully. After five minutes of heating, stir the curd from the bottom of the kettle raising it toward the top. Stir the curd for one minute and check the temperature; the temperature of the curd should have increased only about one degree during these first five minutes. Continue heating the curd, stirring it for one minute every four minutes; stirring the curd allows it to heat uniformly and prevents it from sticking together. The temperature should be increasing about one degree per minute after ten minutes of cooking. The total time to raise the curd to 100 degrees should be about thirty-five to forty minutes.

When the temperature of the curd reaches 100 degrees, increase the heat and stir it for one minute every two minutes. Heat the curds and whey to 115 degrees. This should take about fifteen minutes. At 115 degrees, turn down the heat so that the curd will stay at the same temperature. Maintain this temperature for twenty to thirty minutes, stirring constantly. After twenty minutes, begin testing the curd for firmness.

Test the curd by lifting several pieces out of the kettle on your fingertip. Very gently pinch the curd between the thumb and forefinger. The curd should feel slightly resilient when compressed and should not break or rupture easily. Only experience can truly describe what a properly firm curd is, the point being somewhere between mushy and hard. When you have decided that the curd is firm enough, you may want to double check. Remove about one-half teaspoon of curd from the kettle and place it into a glass of ice water. After it has thoroughly chilled, remove it and compare its firmness to the commercial product. They should be roughly the same.

If you find that you have not gotten a firm enough curd after thirty minutes at 115 degrees, raise the temperature to 120 or even 125 degrees. Do not go above 125, however.

When the curd is firm enough, remove the kettle with the curd from the water bath and place it next to the sink. With a clean cup, dip the whey out of the kettle down to the level of the curd. Place the colander into the sink and cover it with several layers of cheesecloth. Pour the remaining curds and whey onto the cheesecloth and let it drain for two or three minutes.

While the curd is draining, pour the hot water out of the outer kettle and refill it with cold water. Gather the corners of the cheesecloth containing the curd to form a bag around it. Dip the bag of curd into the cold water to rinse the whey from the curd and to cool it. Raise and lower the bag in the water and very gently work the curd inside the bag to be sure the cool water is reaching all the curd. Continue rinsing the curd for three minutes, then return the curd to the colander and pour out the water. Refill the kettle with cold water and add a tray full of ice cubes to the water.

Now gather up the cheesecloth again and immerse the bag of curd into the ice water. Rinse and chill the curd for five minutes, working the curd around in the bag to insure even and thorough cooling of the curd. After all of the curd is thoroughly chilled, remove the bag from the ice water and return it to the colander for draining. Allow the curd to drain for at least an hour or until the whey stops draining. Shake the colander occasionally to prevent the curd from matting.

What you have now is unsalted cottage cheese, a slightly acid and delicious product, especially for those on salt-free diets. If you prefer salted cottage cheese, transfer the drained curd to a mixing bowl and stir in one and one-half teaspoons of salt (adjust to taste). Now you have a high protein, low fat, low calorie food which is an excellent addition to any diet. If you can stand the calories, the cottage cheese can be creamed by adding a quarter cup of milk, half-and-half, or cream to the salted curd and stirring it in thoroughly. Cottage cheese should be eaten as fresh as possible and can be served immediately.

LARGE CURD COTTAGE CHEESE

Large curd cottage cheese is the low acid version of cottage cheese. It takes less time to make, is sweeter and gives a slightly larger yield than the small curd version.

In addition to skimmed milk and starter, you will need rennet to make large curd cheese. If you obtained rennet compounded for one gallon lots of milk, you will use one whole tablet; if you have commercial rennet, you will have to dilute it according to the manufacturer's recommendations and use only enough for one gallon.

Add one gallon of skimmed milk to the inner kettle of the cheese cooking assembly. Place warm water into the outer kettle until the level of the water is the same as that of the milk. Apply heat to the water and raise the temperature of the milk to 72°. Stir in one-quarter cup of fresh cultured buttermilk. Dissolve the rennet tablet in a tablespoon of cool water and stir it into the milk. Set the kettle in a place where the milk will remain at 72 to 80 degrees. It may be necessary to reheat the water to maintain this temperature. Cover the kettle and let it stand undisturbed for twelve to eighteen hours.

Test the milk for coagulation by inserting a knife into the curd at the side of the kettle. Using the side of the knife, gently pull the curd toward the center of the kettle. The curd should break cleanly away from the side of the kettle and have the consistency of pudding.

With the exception of adding rennet, the preparation of large curd cheese is almost identical with that of small curd. The major difference between the two is the time required to coagulate the milk. Large curd cheese requires about six hours less time to coagulate. The shorter coagulation time allows less acid to develop before the curd is cut; yielding a softer and sweeter curd.

Cut the curd into five-eighths-inch cubes and let the curd stand for four minutes. Now use a large spoon and very gently stir the curd by lifting the curd from the bottom of the kettle and raising it to the top. Stir in this manner for about one minute. Allow the curd to stand for four more minutes and then stir again.

Slowly heat the water in the outer kettle until the temperature of the curd reaches 110 degrees. Try to maintain an even temperature rise of 1 degree per minute. It may take five minutes for the first 1-degree rise, this is normal and desirable; thereafter, a 1-degree rise per minute should not be difficult to maintain. Stir the curd for one minute every four minutes as you heat the curd. At 110 degrees the curd should be sufficiently firm, if not, the curd may be heated to 115 or even 120 degrees. Test the curd for proper firmness by squeezing it gently between the thumb and forefinger. It should be somewhat resilient, neither mushy nor hard.

When the curd is sufficiently firm, dip off the whey with a measuring cup down to the level of the curd. Pour the remaining whey and curds into a colander lined with several layers of cheesecloth. Let the curd drain for three minutes.

Pour the hot water from the outer kettle and refill it with

cold water. Gather the corners of the cheesecloth together to form a bag around the curd and dip the bag into the cold water. Work the curd gently inside the bag to make sure the water reaches all of the curd. After three minutes, remove the bag of curd from the water and return it to the colander to drain. Pour out the water and refill the kettle with fresh cold water. Add a tray of ice cubes to the water. Gather up the corners of the cheesecloth bag and immerse the curd into the ice water. Move the bag up and down in the water and work the curd gently with your hand. Rinse the curd until it is all thoroughly chilled, about five minutes. Remove the curd from the water and return it to the colander for draining. Allow the curd to drain until the whey stops dripping, about one and one-half hours. Shake the colander occasionally to prevent the curd from sticking together.

After draining, the curd is ready for consumption. If you prefer salted curd, transfer the curd to a mixing bowl and stir in salt at the rate of one teaspoon for every pound of drained curd. For creamed cottage cheese, add two ounces of milk or cream per pound of drained curd. Mix salt and cream in thoroughly and serve while very fresh.

Now that you have made and eaten your own cottage cheese, you should be glowing with the light of a brilliant success. This could well be the best cottage cheese you have eaten since the days your mother made it on the farm. There is, unfortunately, a possibility, although slight, that your product is not good. If your cottage cheese has developed a fault, that's cheese maker's talk for "no good," I will try to give you some idea as to what went wrong. Don't give up too easily, even the best cooks turn out a flop once in a while.

If your cheese has a "sour, acid flavor," too much acid developed before and while cooking. Next time, try using a little more starter and/or heat the curd slightly faster after cutting the curd. It may be that the curd was simply not cooked long enough. Undercooking leaves too much whey inside the curd giving it a sour taste. The last possibility may be insufficient washing. Be certain that the rinse water penetrates all the way through the curd removing as much whey as possible.

Yeasty, sweet, or moldy flavors are almost always the result of unsanitary conditions. Unclean utensils, contaminated starter, or milk which has not been completely pasteurized can introduce yeast, milk, and undesirable bacteria into the cheese. The warm temperature needed to make cheese is also ideal for yeast and bacteria growth. To avoid this problem, sterilize everything except your thermometer. Wash the thermometer very carefully but do not overheat it.

A tough, dry curd is usually the result of too much cooking. Try to remember what the curd felt like when you tested it and stop cooking before it feels the same way the next time or cut ten minutes off of the cooking time you used. It is also possible that the curd may have been cut too finely; use one-quarter-inch cuts for small curd and five-eighths-inch cuts for large curd. If the curd is also lacking in flavor, it may be that insufficient acid developed while ripening the milk; try using less starter in future batches.

These problems are common to all varieties of cheese, so it is a good idea to keep them in mind when sampling any of your own cheese.

NEUFCHÂTEL CHEESE

In France there is a region where pasture land is exceptionally fine and, therefore, also the cattle and their milk products. It is from this area that the original Neufchâtel first came. Neufchâtel is made from whole milk; it is made with very little rennet and a long acid developing time. It is lightly salted and, when fresh, resembles cream cheese. Aged Neufchâtel is quite firm and has a pungent flavor.

Place one gallon of whole milk into the inner container of the cheese cooking assembly and heat it to 82 to 86 degrees. Stir in four tablespoons of fresh cultured buttermilk. Use one half the amount of rennet recommended for one gallon of milk. Dissolve the rennet in two tablespoons of cool water and stir half of this solution into the milk. Hold the temperature, as near as possible, at 85 degrees. The milk should coagulate in sixteen to eighteen hours.

Place a colander in the sink and line it with very fine cheesecloth or muslin. Muslin is the better choice since the curd is not cooked and is very soft and runny. I have found that most cheesecloth available through hardware stores is far too coarse for uncooked curd. Be certain to use a plain white material and boil it for five minutes.

Test the milk for coagulation. When the milk is coagulated, pour the contents of the kettle into the colander and allow it to drain for two to four hours.

When the curd has almost completely stopped dripping, gather the corners of the material to form a bag around the curd. Tie the opposite corners together and draw them together so that the curd cannot leak out. Surround the bag of curd with ice to chill the curd. When the curd is thoroughly chilled, remove it from the ice. Place the bag of curd on a board and place a second board on top of it. Place two bricks on top for weight. Set the whole thing into a cake pan to catch the whey and place it into the refrigerator for eight hours.

Remove the bag of curd from the refrigerator and cut it open. Remove the curd from the bag and place it into a mixing bowl. Add about one and one-half teaspoons of salt and knead it into the curd with your hands. Any large lumps which may have formed should now be broken up.

The cheese should now be pressed lightly in your cheese press. Cut two squares of sterilized muslin about one inch larger than your round pressing discs. Place one of your discs on a hard, flat surface and cover it with one of the cloth squares. Take the cylinder and force it down over the cloth-covered disc; the edges of the cloth should hang out of the end of the cylinder. Place the cylinder, closed end down, onto a wire cake cooling rack. Spoon the salted curd into the press. Place the second square of cloth over the open end of the cylinder. Place the second disc on the cylinder and force it inside with the cloth acting as a seal around the edges. Push the disc evenly down on top of the curd. Place a jar inside of the cylinder; the jar should stick out of the press at least one inch. Place a brick on top of the jar, and press the curd in the refrigerator for forty-eight hours.

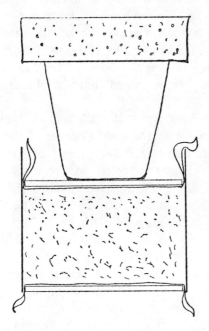

Figure 4. The cheese pressing arrangement for Neufchâtel.

Remove the press from the refrigerator and carefully pry out the lower disc (the one at the end of the cylinder). Peel the cloth off of the cheese and push the cheese out of the press and onto a plate using the other disc. Rub salt lightly on the outside of the cheese and allow it to dry for twenty-four hours at room temperature. After drying, place the cheese in the most humid part of your refrigerator for three to four weeks. Turn the cheese over every day and salt it again after one week. Neufchâtel can also be eaten fresh, without curing, and will be very much like cream cheese.

CREAM CHEESE

Almost everyone is familiar with cream cheese. It comes neatly foil wrapped in compact bricks from the supermarket. It is the basic ingredient in cheesecake, cheese dips, and cake frosting, and a delicious filling in Danish pastry. It is highly perishable and loaded with calories. Over 125 million pounds of cream cheese are consumed annually, attesting to its popularity.

The cream cheese we will make will be somewhat richer than commercial cream cheese. Because of the high cost of cream we will also use only a quart of material. Cream cheese is very lightly renneted and requires a fairly long ripening time. What you make your cheese from will determine how rich the final cream cheese will be. Half-and-half will make a cream cheese a little lower in butterfat than that required to legally be called cream cheese. Whipping cream will produce a cream cheese of the "Petit-Suisse" variety.

To make cream cheese place one quart of half-and-half into a saucepan. To this add one-half pint of whipping cream. The whipping cream is needed to increase the butterfat content of the total mixture. Very gently heat the cream to 72 degrees, then stir in one tablespoon of cultured buttermilk. Dissolve the rennet in one cup of cool water. When completely dissolved, add one-fourth teaspoon of the rennet solution to the cream. The rennet can be left out altogether; however, a somewhat lower yield will result.

Cover the container and place it where the temperature will stay at about 72 degrees. With rennet the cream should set in about twelve to sixteen hours; without rennet, the cream should set in about eighteen hours.

"To cook or not to cook, that is the question." Two different methods of preparing the curd seem to share equal popularity so I will present both of them. I have used both with success. The uncooked variety may take several days to drain, however, and if you need the cheese for tomorrow's party, you may want to use the speedier cooked curd method.

To prepare cream cheese by cooking the curd, place the kettle with the coagulated cream into a pan of water. Heat the water slowly to raise the temperature of the curd to 130 degrees. Stir the curd gently with a spoon. Hold the curd at 130 degrees for forty-five minutes. The mixture will be like a thick soup when it is hot, but it will thicken again as it cools. Allow the curd to cool slowly to 90 degrees and stir in one tablespoon of salt. After salting, place the kettle in the refrigerator and chill the mixture to 40 degrees. Chilling the curd will take about four or five hours.

A draining bag is a useful accessory for preparing cream cheeses. To make one, cut a rectangle of white muslin about nine inches by eighteen inches. Fold the material in half and sew up the two sides forming a bag. Leave the top open and use the bag with the seam to the outside. Sterilize the bag by boiling in water for five minutes.

Hold the draining bag over the sink and pour the chilled curd into it. Close the bag by wrapping a rubber band around it as close to the level of the cheese as possible. Allow the curd to drain for about two hours or until the whey has nearly stopped dripping. Squeeze the bag gently to force out the excess whey and to speed up the draining. Fill a colander one-half full with ice cubes and place the colander in a shallow pan. Place the bag of curd on the ice and place an inverted saucer on top of the bag. Place a brick or some other heavy object on top of the saucer. Fill the remaining space in the colander with as much ice as possible and place the whole thing into the refrigerator for draining. Allow it to drain for about twenty-four hours. Remove the curd from the bag and place it in a jar or plastic container with a lid. Cream cheese is highly perishable and must be kept refrigerated; it should not be kept for more than three weeks, in any case. Keep in mind that the cheese which you will be preparing at home contain no preservatives, emulsifiers, stabilizers, or anti-bacterial agents and, therefore, will mold, spoil, or separate much more readily than the store-bought equivalent. Proper refrigeration and cleanliness are very important.

When following the method in which the curd is not cooked, the curd is drained after it is coagulated. Test the curd for coagulation and when it is set, break up the curd with a spoon. Line a colander with muslin and pour the curd into the colander. Allow it to drain for about one hour. Gather up the four corners of the muslin, two in each hand, and tie the ends in each hand together. In this way, a tight bag is formed around the curd.

Half fill a deep bowl with ice and place the curd in the bag on the ice. Place a plate on the bag and set a brick on the plate to apply a small amount of pressure on the curd. Cover the bag and plate with ice and allow the curd to drain until it is as dry as commercial cream cheese (twenty-four to forty-eight hours). Keep ice around the bag to keep the curd chilled until it is dry. When it is sufficiently drained, remove it from the bag and place it into a plastic container having a sealable lid. Stir in about one and one-half teaspoons of salt or according to taste. Close the container and store in the refrigerator until ready to serve. Cream cheese should be used as fresh as possible and should not be kept longer than three weeks.

CULTURED CREAM (Sour Cream)

Cultured cream or sour cream is as common as catsup in some kitchens. Sour cream can be used as a dressing on fruits and vegetables, as a spread on rye and whole wheat bread, on prepared cereals, as a salad dressing, mixed with herbs and spices, and, of course, as a favorite topping on baked potatoes. Sour cream, like cream cheese, can be made in varying degrees of richness and calories. Using half-and-half will produce a relatively low calorie version, and adding whipping cream will increase the calories and creaminess in proportion. Besides all of this, sour cream is easy to make. Sour cream does not keep well and, therefore, we will make only one pint. If you wish to make a larger quantity, simply increase the proportions.

Sterilize two half-pint canning jars and lids and cool them for use later. Mix one half pint of whipping cream with one cup of whole milk in a clean bowl. Stir in one tablespoon plus two teaspoons of fresh cultured buttermilk. Fill each half-pint jar and turn on the lids. Place the jars where they will stay at 72 degrees for sixteen to eighteen hours. It is important that the temperature does not become too cold.

The cream could be well coagulated after sixteen hours. Stir up the cream in each jar and place in the refrigerator for forty-eight hours. The sour cream is now ready for use and should be consumed within one week. Add salt or other flavorings just before serving.

NOTHIN'-TO-IT CHEESE—IN THREE FLAVORS

Making this cheese is particularly well suited to warm climates or summer months. It requires no cooking and no rennet. It can be made with just about any milk and cream combination that appeals to you. It can be seasoned, spiced, or liqueured depending on its final use. And finally, it is very good.

Start with one-half gallon of skim or whole milk or a quart of cream or a combination of milk and cream totaling one-half gallon. Pour the milk into a kettle and heat it to 95 degrees. Remove it from the heat and stand the kettle in a warm place. Stir in one-quarter cup of fresh cultured buttermilk (use only two tablespoons if you are using all cream) and cover the kettle. The curd should develop in twenty-four to forty-eight hours.

Place a layer of muslin into a colander and set it into the sink. Pour the coagulated milk into the colander and let it drain for about twenty minutes. Place the colander into a kettle for further draining. There should be at least three inches under the colander to keep the curd out of the whey which will accumulate. Place the kettle and colander into a plastic bag and close the end with a wire tie or rubber band. Now place the kettle, colander, and bag into the refrigerator for twenty-four hours.

After draining for twenty-four hours the cheese is ready to be flavored or spiced. Remove the cheese from the bag and discard the whey. Place the cheese into a mixing bowl and let your imagination run wild. I will give you three suggestions but your own imagination and taste will give you dozens more.

Plain Cheese
This sounds like a cop-out on one flavor, but this cheese is excellent with only a little salt added. After salting, the cheese must be drained further. Stir in three-quarters teaspoon salt. Spoon about one cup of the salted cheese onto a square of fine cheesecloth, tie the corners of the cloth together to

form a bag and place on a wire cooling rack. Repeat this until all the cheese is used up. The small quantity of cheese in a bag is to insure that the cheese drains properly. Place the cooling rack on a cake pan. Put the pan and rack back into the plastic bag and return to the refrigerator for twenty-four to forty-eight hours.

After draining, remove the bag from the refrigerator and place the cheese into serving bowls, removing the cheesecloth from the cheese. At room temperature this cheese is soft and spreadable; however, it is also perishable and should be kept refrigerated until ready to use. Also, it should be eaten as fresh as possible, within a week's time.

Sweet Cheese

For this flavor, stir in one-quarter teaspoon of salt, two tablespoons of powdered sugar, and one ounce of crème de menthe, and drain it the same way as the plain cheese. Instead of crème de menthe, you can use any liqueur that turns you on. Kahlua would be fascinating and crème de cocoa should make it into a dessert-type treat. The sweet cheese is excellent when combined with gelatin or a fruit salad.

Tangy Cheese

This flavor is great for the party goer. Stir thoroughly into the cheese one-quarter teaspoon Worchestershire sauce, one-quarter teaspoon salt, eight drops of Tabasco, one and one-half teaspoons chili powder, and one-quarter teaspoon Maggi seasoning. Chop up four cloves of garlic and one cup of hickory nuts and mix these into the seasoned cheese. Drain the cheese the same way as the plain cheese. This flavor can be used as a spread or a dip and is guaranteed to keep vampires out of your bedroom.

If you have made all the cheeses detailed in this chapter, you probably feel like a semi-professional cheese maker. Now that your confidence is built up to a high level, you can probably stand the frustration of trying to produce a perfect Cheddar or edible mozzarella. The cheeses that follow are not difficult to make but they are difficult to make right, especially in the small quantities with which we must work. A cheese factory makes Cheddar from 10,000 pounds of milk in a single vat and it is difficult to overcook half a ton of curd. A pound of curd is much easier to overcook and overcooking produces a tough and dry cheese. But you *will* produce good cheese and it will be all your own.

4
COLBY, MONTEREY, CHEDDAR, AND CARAWAY CHEESE

Before starting on the non-cream-type cheeses, I would like to discuss lactic starters. By this time you should pretty well know whether you are going to enjoy making cheese. Using buttermilk as a starter will cause milk to acidify and cheese will be produced but making a specific type of cheese, which will taste, feel, and ripen in a predictable manner requires the use of specific starter organisms. In Chapter 2 I mentioned two organisms found in lactic cultures. These are the organisms necessary to produce Cheddar, brick, Colby, Edam, Gouda, and many other cheeses; these organisms and several others are present in buttermilk. It is these "other" organisms which give buttermilk its distinctive flavor but they are not necessary or desirable in cheese. A pure strain of organisms will form acid in milk at a predictably high rate and allows cheese making to become a time-controlled procedure. Unless you wish to invest in equipment to titrate whey acidity, making cheese by the clock has definite advantages.

Italian and Swiss cheese and yogurt are made from strains

of organisms not found in buttermilk. Yogurt contains *Lacto-bacillus bulgaricus* and *Streptococcus thermophilus* and Italian and Swiss cheeses are made with starters containing a mixture of these two organisms. Swiss, in addition, must have propionic acid bacteria present; these bacteria convert lactic acid into propionic and acetic acid which give Swiss its "nutty" flavor.

Whenever possible, I will name a commercial product which should prove suitable as a starter material and also will name the specific organisms. If you decide to grow your own cultures, refer to Appendix 1 at the end of this book for specific instructions on growing them and how to obtain the cultures.

COLBY CHEESE

Colby is a very popular midwestern cheese which is similar to Cheddar but with a higher moisture content and the curd is not matted or milled. Colby has a soft body and open texture and for these reasons does not keep as well as Cheddar. It is named after the town in which it was first made, Colby, Wisconsin. It can be made from either raw or pasteurized whole milk, however, pasteurized milk will give much better control over the final quality and minimize faults from undesirable bacteria.

Pour one gallon of fresh, whole milk into the inner kettle of the cheese cooking assembly and add warm water to the outer container to the level of the milk. Heat the water slowly until the milk is 88 degrees. Do not heat the water too rapidly because you do not want the milk to get too warm. When you have stabilized the milk at 88 degrees, you are ready to add the starter. To the warm milk add four ounces of lactic starter or six to eight ounces of buttermilk and note the time. Hold the temperature as nearly constant as possible for the next one and one-half hours.

After adding the starter, stir the milk continuously for two minutes; then stir the milk every two minutes for the next half hour. The time after adding the starter is the ripening period. The acid-producing organisms are now increasing the acid content of the milk about four one-hundreths of 1 per cent. One-half hour after adding the starter prepare to color the milk.

Place two tablespoons of cool water into a small container and dissolve a cheese color tablet in it. Pour the coloring material into the milk while stirring vigorously. Continue stirring the milk intermittently for another fifteen minutes.

Forty-five minutes after adding the starter prepare to add the rennet. Crush and dissolve the rennet in one tablespoon of cool, soft water and add it to the milk immediately. Rennet is very sensitive to hard water and should not, therefore, be allowed to stand in water solution for long periods of time. Hard water can destroy the effectiveness of rennet in a few minutes. Stir the milk continuously for the next three minutes and then stop. Remove all utensils from the milk and let it stand undisturbed until it is set firmly. This should take twenty to thirty minutes from the time the rennet is added. Test the milk for coagulation thirty minutes after adding the rennet. The temperature should still be 88 degrees.

Cut the curd into three-eighths-inch cubes and then let it stand undisturbed for fifteen minutes. Be certain that the temperature remains at 88 degrees.

Fifteen minutes after cutting the curd, start heating the curd very gently. It should take ten minutes for the temperature to increase 2 degrees. During this time use a spoon to turn the curd over in the kettle; the curd should not be stirred but raised from the bottom of the kettle to prevent it from overheating and agitated sufficiently to keep the curd from sticking together. Continue heating the curd slowly to 94 degrees during the next ten minutes; continue turning the curd over gently in the kettle. The last ten minutes of heating should bring the temperature to 100 to 102 degrees. Under no circumstances should 102 degrees be exceeded since this will cause the curd to become excessively dry. Turn the heat down soon enough to prevent the temperature from rising too high. Hold the temperature between 100 and 102 degrees for one hour, stirring only enough to prevent matting or overheating of the curd on the bottom.

After cooking the curd allow it to settle for a minute or two. Use a measuring cup to bail the whey out of the cooking kettle down to the level of the curd. Fill a pitcher with cold water and pour it into the curd, stirring continuously, until the temperature is lowered to 80 degrees. The temperature to which the curd is cooled will have a strong influence on the moisture content of the finished cheese. If your finished cheese is wet and weak-bodied, try lowering the temperature to 88 degrees in this step. If it is too dry, the curd may be cooled to as low as 70 degrees. Stir the curd continuously, but slowly, for fifteen minutes, maintaining a constant temperature.

Pour the curd into a colander and let it drain for twenty minutes. Keep the curd covered with a warm, wet towel to prevent the curd from drying and to keep it warm. Stir the curd frequently to prevent the curd from matting. After draining, stir three to five teaspoons of salt per pound of curd into the curd. Use a coarse salt, such as canning salt; never use iodized salt. Add the salt in three steps to allow time for the previously applied salt to dissolve. When the curd is salted, allow it to stand for another twenty minutes to insure that all of the salt is dissolved and to allow any further whey to drain. Keep the curd covered to prevent drying and stir occasionally to avoid matting.

While the curd is draining, prepare your cheese press to receive the curd. Place one of the discs inside of the cylinder and place the cylinder on a flat surface. Push the disc to the bottom of the cylinder. Prepare an eighteen-inch square double layer of cheesecloth, and push it into the cylinder evenly, allowing the ends to hang over the edge of the cylinder. Turn a wing nut onto the threaded rod, and lay it aside.

When the curd has finished draining, spoon the curd into the cylinder and press it down with your fist. When the cylinder is full, pick it up with the disc in place and insert the threaded rod through the cheese until the wing nut is against the bottom disc.

Fold the cheesecloth around the rod, at the open end, and trim off any excess cloth. Place the second disc over the rod and slide it into the cylinder. Place the second wing nut on the rod and turn it down against the plate. Tighten the wing nuts moderately by hand. Let the cylinder lay on its side for fifteen minutes and then tighten the nuts firmly. Whey will drain from the cylinder throughout the pressing process, so it is a good idea to keep the cylinder in a sink. Allow the cheese to drain in the press for three to five hours after full pressure has been applied.

When the pressing is complete, remove the cheese from the press. Remove the rod from the cheese and remove the cheesecloth. Wrap the cheese in a fresh, single layer of cheesecloth, wrapping it as neatly and uniformly as possible. Place the finished cheese into the high humidity compartment of your refrigerator. A meat storage box or vegetable crisper usually has fairly high humidity. Let the cheese air-dry in the refrigerator overnight or until it is dry to the touch.

Melt about one-quarter pound of paraffin in a double boiler. Be very careful with melted paraffin near open flames since it can ignite if it is overheated. Using a double boiler or water bath will prevent overheating. Remove the cheese from the refrigerator and dip it into the melted paraffin until it is completely sealed in the wax. Place a label on your cheese describing the type and the date and return it to the refrigerator for curing. Cure the cheese for at least three weeks at 50 degrees; use longer curing times at lower temperatures. Colby does not keep as well as Cheddar and should be consumed within three months.

MONTEREY CHEESE

Monterey was first made about 1892 in Monterey County, California. Monterey, also known as Jack, can be made from skim, part skim, or whole milk. Whole milk Monterey is a semisoft cheese, whereas, Monterey made from skimmed milk is hard enough for grating. It is made with a process very similar to Colby. This cheese is very popular on the West Coast as an appetizer and in cooking.

Pour one gallon of whole, pasteurized milk into the inner kettle of the cheese cooking assembly and add warm water to the outer container to the level of the milk. Heat the water slowly to bring the temperature of the milk to 88 degrees. When the milk is at 88 degrees the starter may be added. To the warm milk add four ounces of lactic starter or six to eight ounces of buttermilk. The temperature of the milk must be kept at 88 degrees for the next one and one-half hours.

Stir the milk continuously for two minutes after adding the starter and then stir the milk vigorously every two minutes for the next forty-five minutes.

Forty-five minutes after adding the starter prepare to add the rennet. Dissolve the rennet in one tablespoon of cool, soft water and stir it vigorously into the milk. Continue stirring the milk for three minutes and then remove all of the utensils from the milk. Let the milk stand undisturbed for twenty to thirty minutes or until it is firmly set. Test the milk for coagulation and check to see that the temperature is still 88 degrees.

After the milk has coagulated, cut the curd into three-eighths-inch cubes and let it stand undisturbed for fifteen minutes. Avoid making excessively fine cuts through the curd; it is better to have some larger lumps of curd initially than fine particles. The large lumps can be cut up while stirring the curd, but the fine particles will usually be lost during the draining process and so reduce the yield. The finer curd usually will also produce a dryer cheese which will tend to crumble when cut.

Start heating the curd very gently. Initially, only 1 degree rise in five minutes is desirable. After ten minutes heat the curd at the rate of 2 degrees every five minutes. This heating schedule should bring the curd to 94 degrees after twenty minutes of cooking. The final ten minutes of cooking should raise the temperature to 100 to 102 degrees. It is better to hold the lower temperature for the first batch of cheese to prevent excessive drying. If the cheese is too wet after pressing the temperature can be raised for future batches; nothing is so disappointing as a cheese which is dry and crumbly when it should be smooth and creamy. While cooking the curd a spoon should be used to raise the curd from the bottom of the kettle to the top. Stir the curd, in this way, only enough to keep the curd from sticking together or overheating. Excessive stirring will also tend to produce a dryer curd. Hold the curd at 100 degrees for one hour.

After cooking the curd allow it to settle for about two minutes. Fill the sink with about five inches of cold tap water. Lift the inner kettle with the curd out of the hot water and place it into the sink. Stir the curd gently but continuously until the temperature has been lowered to 86 degrees. Remove the curd kettle from the cold water and set it aside. Wrap the kettle with several heavy towels to prevent any further cooling of the curd. Stir the curd gently for fifteen minutes while maintaining the temperature at 86 degrees.

If the temperature varies from 86 degrees the kettle can be immersed in either the hot water or the cold water until it remains at 86 degrees.

Pour the curd into a colander and let it drain for twenty minutes. Keep the curd warm and moist by covering the colander with a warm, wet towel. Stir the curd frequently to prevent it from matting. After draining, transfer the curd to a mixing bowl and stir three to five teaspoons of salt into the curd. Let the curd stand for twenty minutes or until all of the salt is completely dissolved. Keep the curd covered to avoid drying and stir frequently to prevent matting.

Prepare a square piece of muslin large enough to hold all of the curd. Spoon the curd onto the muslin and draw up the corners and sides of the muslin bag until the bag can be tied to keep the curd from escaping. Tie the bag securely and form the cheese into a spherical shape. Place the bag on a clean hardwood board and place a second board on top of the bag, flattening the cheese. Place sufficient weight on the top board to compress the cheese to one third to one half of its original height. The knot in the bag will make the typical center indentation found in Monterey cheese. Press the cheese for twenty-four hours and then remove the boards. Monterey should be cured for three to six weeks at 60 degrees and 70 per cent relative humidity. If a lower temperature must be used the curing time will be proportionately longer. The humidity should be kept fairly high to prevent drying. If the Monterey is to be used for grating it must be cured for at least six months. Seal the cheese in paraffin while curing if drying cannot be prevented.

CHEDDAR CHEESE

Cheddar is probably the most popular cheese in the United States. It has been known for half a millennium. Cheddar is made from whole milk and ranges in flavor from mild to sharp depending on how long it has ripened. Cheddar is a common ingredient in many dishes and cheese spreads.

Cheddar cheese is made following a process very similar to Colby except Cheddar curd is matted or fused together, then it is milled or broken up before it is pressed into a solid mass. Cheddar is a fairly difficult cheese to make because temperature must be precisely controlled. It is worth trying to make because good Cheddar is not always easy to find. The total making time for Cheddar is about six hours, so plan your time accordingly.

Begin by placing one gallon of whole milk into the inner kettle of your cheese cooking assembly. Add water to the outer kettle to the level of the milk and slowly heat it to 88 degrees. When the temperature has been adjusted so that the milk will remain at exactly 88 the starter can be added. Note the time and add two tablespoons of lactic starter or five tablespoons of buttermilk. Stir the starter into the milk vigorously for five minutes then stir the milk every five minutes for a minute.

Thirty minutes after adding the starter add cheese coloring to the milk. Dissolve the color tablet in about two tablespoons of cool water and stir it vigorously into the milk. Continue stirring the milk every five minutes. Remember that it is not necessary to color your cheese. If for some reason you do not wish to add any coloring material to your cheese, simply omit it. The resulting cheese will not taste any different from its colored brother; however, there may be some psychological obstacles to overcome when tasting stark, white Cheddar cheese.

Fifteen minutes after adding the coloring material the rennet should be added. Dissolve the rennet in about two tablespoons of cool water and stir it immediately into the milk. Note the time you add the rennet, it should be forty-five minutes since adding the starter. Stir the milk continuously, and vigorously, for five minutes then stop, remove all of the utensils except the thermometer from the kettle and let it stand undisturbed for thirty minutes or until it is firmly coagulated. Test the curd for proper development thirty minutes after adding the rennet.

Cut the curd into one-quarter-inch strips and then cut these strips into one-quarter-inch squares. Do not make the angle cuts through the curd because this will tend to make the curd too fine and hence, too dry.

Fifteen minutes after cutting the curd, increase the heat slightly. The temperature should increase only one degree, to 89 degrees, during the first five minutes of cooking. Use a large spoon to turn the curd over from the top to the bottom of the kettle. Use the spoon to cut through any large pieces of curd. Stir the curd only enough to keep the curd from matting or overheating. Increase the temperature of the curd to 93 degrees during the next ten minutes. Continue stirring the curd very gently and cut up any large curds which come up from the bottom. Raise the temperature three degrees every five minutes until 102 degrees is reached; be certain to lower the heat before the final temperature is reached so that you do not exceed it. Remember that the water in the outer kettle is considerably warmer than the curd by now and will require some time to cool down. A few ice cubes may come in very handy from time to time. Hold the temperature at 102 degrees for one and one-quarter hours. Stir the curd gently and frequently while cooking the curd to prevent overheating.

Place a colander large enough to hold all of the curd into a sink. Lift the cooking kettle from the water and pour the curd into the colander. Let the whey drain for five minutes. Cover the curd with a damp towel to prevent it from drying. While the curd is draining, check the temperature of the hot water in the outer kettle. If it is not 102 degrees, adjust it to that temperature. Wash out the cooking kettle to remove any curd which may have adhered to the sides.

After draining the curd for five minutes return it to the clean cooking kettle. Spread the curd evenly across the bottom of the kettle and place the kettle into the warm water. The water in the outer kettle should be 100 to 102 degrees. Allow the water to cool slowly to 91 degrees during the next one and three-quarter hours. The curd will now mat together into a relatively solid mass. After fifteen minutes remove the cooking kettle from the warm water and carefully pour out any accumulated whey. Dump the matted curd onto your hand and remove it from the kettle. Without breaking the partially matted curd, turn it over and return it to the bottom of the cooking kettle. Place the kettle back into the warm water for another fifteen minutes. Repeat this process, drain, turn and heat, six times. The matting process takes one and three-quarter hours and a large amount of acid is formed during this time.

After matting the curd it is milled or broken up into small pieces and salted. Use a spatula to cut the matted curd into roughly one-half-inch chunks. The curd will be very rubbery at this point and will be squeaky if eaten. Mill and salt the curd while the cooking kettle is in the warm water. Add three to five teaspoons of salt to each pound of curd (one gallon of milk yields about one pound of curd) and stir it in thoroughly. Stir the curd every ten minutes until the salt is completely dissolved.

Prepare the cheese press as described in the section on Colby cheese and spoon the curd into the press. Apply pressure to the curd until the whey starts running out. Gradually increase the pressure, by turning the wing nuts, for fifteen minutes. After fifteen minutes the wing nuts should be as tight as you can turn them by hand. Lay the cheese press on its side and let the whey drain from it for five to twenty hours.

The time is not particularly important and can be adjusted to suit your own time schedule.

After pressing the cheese remove it from the press and place it in the high humidity section of your refrigerator. Some refrigerators have special high-humidity meat keeping compartments; this is an excellent place to keep cheese. A vegetable crisper is also a fairly high-humidity area. Allow the cheese to dry in the refrigerator until the surface is dry, then place the cheese into a plastic bag and seal it tightly. Allow Cheddar to ripen at least three weeks. Cheddar can be kept for up to a year provided you can prevent it from drying out. The longer it ripens, the sharper will be its flavor and the dryer its texture.

CARAWAY CHEESE

Spiced cheeses, such as caraway, are very popular in the Scandinavian countries and many varieties originated there. Besides caraway seed, cumin, anise, pepper, clove, sage, bacon crisps, or pimiento can be added to cheese to lend their special flavors. The amount that is added is strictly a matter of individual taste, however, it is best to use less than you would estimate being enough. About one tablespoonful of caraway seed would be a sufficient quantity for a pound of cheese. Any of the cheeses in this section can be spiced with good results. The spices are stirred into the curd at the same time that salt is added. At least three weeks should be allowed to ripen the cheese and to allow the spice flavor to penetrate throughout the cheese. Your personal culinary genius is the only limiting factor for creating an exciting new spiced cheese.

5

BRICK CHEESE

Brick cheese is one of the very few cheeses that are entirely of American origin. The cheese was first made by John Jossi about 1876 in Richwood, Wisconsin. John moved to a cheese factory near Watertown, Wisconsin, in 1877 where he continued to manufacture his creation under his own direction; brick cheese was made in this factory until 1943.

Brick cheese is the midway point between Cheddar and Limburger. It is softer than Cheddar but harder than Limburger; it is not as sharp as Cheddar nor as strong as Limburger. Its name is probably derived from the fact that bricks were used to press the curd in its form.

With brick cheese we will deviate from the one-gallon formula and substitute a five-gallon recipe. We will also enter the world of difficult-to-make cheese. The making is not really difficult but proper curing is very difficult and some special equipment will have to be gathered. First, you will need a kettle which can hold five gallons of milk. Then you will need a cake cooling rack and two very large salad bowls (these should be the same size so that they can be put together to form a special curing chamber). If you are handy with wood, you may wish to build the curing chamber described in Appendix 2.

You will also need a five- by ten-inch straight-sided cake or bread pan about five inches high to serve as a mold and a board just a little smaller than the pan. This board must be able to pass freely through the form when held flat. The mold could also be made from smoothly sanded hardwood using the dimensions given as inside dimensions. If you use a metal pan be sure to cut the bottom out of the pan so that you have only a rectangular frame left.

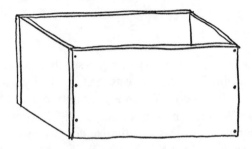

Figure 5. A brick cheese mold.

Lastly, you will need lactic starter culture, *S. thermophilus* culture and *Bacterium linens*. Buttermilk can be substituted for lactic starter and yogurt can be used instead of *S. thermophilus* but *B. linens* just cannot be had except as *B. linens*. It is this bacteria, together with natural yeasts, which give brick cheese its particular flavor.

The first thing you must do to make brick cheese is to buy a small piece of *aged* brick. Pick a piece that has a good mold growth on the outer surface of a reddish brown color. It is from this piece of cheese that you will obtain your *B. linens* and yeasts.

Since I am recommending the use of five gallons of milk

for a single cheese it may be a good time to add some information on the milk itself. Cheese is not made from Grade A milk. Grade A signifies milk processes for consumption as a fluid beverage and the extra precautions are not necessary when the milk is to be processed in food preparation. Grade B milk is used for cheese, it is wholesome and pure, but considerably cheaper. A bit of hunting around for a source of Grade B milk will cut your milk bills by more than half and probably get you fresher milk as an extra value. Buy milk of from 3 to 3½ per cent butterfat. More than 3½ per cent butterfat usually will not produce a good cheese.

Boil a half-pint of water and pour it into a sterile jar. Allow the water to cool to 80 degrees. Cut a piece of rind off of the cheese about one inch square and one-quarter-inch deep. Place the piece of rind into the warm water and mash it in the water. Dissolve as much of the cheese as possible. Strain the water through a piece of cheesecloth and save the water to inoculate your cheese.

Place five gallons of milk into a large kettle and heat it to 90 degrees. Stir the milk continuously while heating to prevent scorching. When the temperature has stabilized add five tablespoons of lactic culture and five tablespoons of *S. thermophilus* culture. Instead of cultures you can substitute three-quarters cup of cultured buttermilk and one-half cup of yogurt. Add the half-pint of water containing *B. linens* and stir these all into the milk vigorously for ten minutes. Turn off any heat under the kettle and wrap the kettle in a towel to retain its warmth.

Dissolve enough rennet for *six* gallons of milk in about one-half cup of soft water. Brick cheese requires slightly more rennet than other cheeses so use the extra amount. Pour the rennet into the milk while stirring vigorously. Stir the milk for five minutes after adding the rennet; the larger volume of milk you use the more important thorough distribution of the rennet in the milk becomes. Five minutes after adding the rennet stop stirring and remove all of the utensils from the kettle. The milk should be ready to cut in about thirty minutes. Test the curd to be certain it is ready for cutting.

Cut the curd into three-eighths-inch cubes and allow them to rest for five minutes. Stir the curd very gently with a large wooden spoon. If any large particles come up from the bottom, be sure to cut them into smaller pieces. Stir the curd occasionally for twenty minutes following cutting. After twenty minutes remove the towel and begin to heat the curd.

Heat the curd very slowly so that 106 degrees is reached in not less than forty-five minutes. Stir the curd from the bottom of the kettle frequently to prevent overheating during the heating process. Stir very gently but with enough force to move the curd away from the heated area at bottom. Stir the curd continuously after the temperature has reached 102 degrees. When the temperature reaches 106 degrees stir continuously for five additional minutes. Stop stirring and let the curd settle to the bottom of the kettle. Be certain that the heat is turned off or very low to prevent overcooking at this time.

When the curd has settled, bail off the whey until there is about one inch of whey above the surface of the curd. Stir the curd in the whey for ten minutes or until the curd has a slightly elastic feel; the curd should be neither mushy nor dry. When you judge the curd is ready, prepare to spoon it into the mold.

Place a clean piece of cloth on a drain board and place the five- by ten-inch mold in the center of the cloth. The drain board should have a rippled or ridged surface so that the whey can escape from under the edge of the mold. Dip the curd out of the kettle with a slotted spoon and place it into the mold. All of the curd should fit into the frame; if it does not fit, you probably have undercooked the curd. The curd will shrink as it cooks and undercooked curd will take up more room. When all of the curd is in the mold, smooth it out over the surface and carefully turn the mold upside down on the drain board. The cloth should be used to cover the mold to retain heat and to prevent drying. Turn the mold over after one-half hour and turn it over again after a second one-half hour. Wait one hour and turn it over again; place the pressing board on the curd at this time. Wait another hour, remove the board, turn the mold over, replace the pressing board, and place a brick (approximately five pounds) on the board. Keep the cheese in as warm a room as possible, about 80 degrees, and keep the mold covered with a damp cloth. Let the curd press in the frame for eighteen hours. After pressing prepare to brine the cheese.

Dissolve about two and one-half pounds of canning salt in one gallon of 60-degree water. Remove the cheese from the mold and float it in the brine solution for one day at 55 to 60 degrees; sprinkle salt over the exposed surface. Cover the container with a damp towel to prevent the cheese from drying on its exposed surface. After twenty-four hours, turn the cheese over, sprinkle salt on the exposed side, cover with a damp cloth, and let it stand for another twenty-four hours at 55 to 60 degrees. After forty-eight hours of brining the cheese is ready for curing.

Place the cake cooling rack on or into one of the large salad bowls. If the rack fits inside of the bowl, fill the bowl with water to about one inch below the level of the rack. If the rack rests on the edge of the bowl, fill the bowl three-quarters full of water. Keep the bowl in a room which is about 60 degrees. Place the cheese on the cake rack. Rub the surface of the new cheese with the rind of the aged cheese you purchased. Leave the aged cheese on the rack with the new cheese during the curing process. Cover the rack with the other salad bowl. This will provide a chamber with a relative humidity of about 90 per cent. If there are any large air leaks around the bowl cover them with a damp towel. The cheese will be kept in this chamber for twenty-one days. Every day remove the cheese from the chamber and wash it with a solution of one-half cup of salt in a quart of water. Wash the cheese gently, do not scrub it. Refill the bowl with water if it needs it and turn the cheese over when you return it to the chamber. Be sure to repeat this process daily. After a short time a reddish brown growth will appear on the surface. This shows that normal curing action is taking place. Do not remove this growth during the curing process. After twenty-one days place the cheese in a fairly dry room for two days or until the cheese is dry enough to be wrapped. Wrap the cheese carefully in a plastic bag or seal it with wax and place it in the refrigerator for two months. Keep it in the high-humidity section of the refrigerator. After two months you will have an aromatic, mellow, and soft cheese with a mildly, pungent flavor.

EDAM AND GOUDA CHEESE

EDAM CHEESE

That red-colored cannon ball you saw at the cheese counter last week is Edam cheese. It is named after the town of Edam in Holland. The cheese is a semisoft, sweet curd cheese made from cow's milk. Edam is pleasingly mild with a firm and crumbly body.

Mix five pints of 2 per cent part skim milk with three pints of whole milk in the inner cooking kettle. Place the inner kettle into the outer kettle and add water to the outer kettle to the level of the milk. Heat the water to raise the temperature of the milk to 84 degrees.

When the milk has stabilized at 84 degrees add two tablespoons of lactic starter or four to five tablespoons of buttermilk. Stir the starter into the milk vigorously for five minutes. Stir the milk frequently during the next twenty-five minutes.

One-half hour after adding the starter, add cheese coloring to the milk. Dissolve a color tablet in two tablespoons of cool water and stir into the milk for fifteen minutes. Stir the milk vigorously every two minutes for the next thirty minutes.

Forty-five minutes after adding the coloring prepare to add rennet. Dissolve the rennet in two tablespoons of cool, soft water. Immediately pour the rennet solution into the milk and stir vigorously for five minutes. Remove all of the utensils from the milk and let it stand undisturbed until it is coagulated. This should require about thirty minutes but may take somewhat longer because of the lower setting temperature. The temperature should be held at 84 degrees throughout the process. Test the curd for development after thirty minutes. When it is firmly set, cut the curd.

Cut the curd into one-quarter-inch cubes and then continue cutting the curd until the cubes are about the size of grains of rice. Stir the curd to raise any large lumps from the bottom of the kettle.

Twenty-five minutes after starting to cut the curd allow it to settle to the bottom of the kettle for five minutes. Bail one third to one half of the whey out of the kettle and discard it. Fill a pitcher with hot water from the faucet (150 degrees) and place it next to the cooking kettle. Start stirring the curd gently and gradually pour in the hot water. Add hot water until the curd is 100 degrees and continue stirring the curd at 100 until it becomes firm. This may take as long as thirty minutes and sometimes longer. When the curd is firm, prepare to drain the curd.

Place four layers of cheesecloth into a colander and set the colander into the sink. Pour the curd into the colander and let it drain for about five minutes. Use the palm of your hand to apply pressure to the curd to press out the whey. Keep the curd as warm as possible while draining it. This may be accomplished by placing the colander over the hot water in the cooking kettle and allowing the last of the whey to drain into the water. When the last of the whey has run off, the curd is ready for pressing.

Spoon the curd into your cheese press and compact it as much as possible with your hand while filling the press. When the press is full, apply pressure to the curd; increase the pressure so that full pressure is attained in fifteen minutes. Stand the press on end and let it drain for fifteen minutes. Tighten the wing nuts and turn the press over to drain for another fifteen minutes.

Repeat this process three times, then remove the cheese from the press. Remove the cheesecloth from the cheese and rewrap it in fresh cheesecloth, making the wrapping as smooth as possible. Replace the cheese in the press with a perforated plate on each end but leave out the threaded rod. Stand the press on end and place a block of wood inside the cylinder so that it protrudes from the top of the cylinder. Place about fifteen pounds of weight on top of the block and let it press this way for two hours. After two hours turn the press over and repeat the pressing for three hours. While pressing the cheese, prepare a saturated brine solution.

Place one-half gallon of cold (50 degree) water into a large bowl. Stir canning salt into the water until the salt will no longer dissolve when you add more salt. Add one-half pint of cold water to this solution and save it for brining your cheese. Salt solutions can be saved and used for several batches of cheese.

Remove the cheese from the press. Place the cheese in the brine solution and seal the bowl with plastic food wrap. Place the bowl in the refrigerator for twenty-four hours. After twenty-four hours turn the cheese over in the brine and replace the plastic wrap. Return the bowl to the refrigerator for a second twenty-four hours. After brining the cheese wash it thoroughly, dry it, and seal it in red paraffin. Store it at 50 degrees for two weeks and it is then ready for eating.

GOUDA CHEESE

Gouda is a cheese very similar to Edam except that it contains more fat and is cured for a longer time. Gouda is made from cow's milk with about 4 per cent butterfat content. The cheese is usually shaped into a flattened sphere and coated with red wax. The manufacturing process is similar to Edam with some important variations.

To one gallon of whole milk add one pint of half-and-half. This will yield a milk of approximately 4 per cent butterfat. Heat the milk mixture to 90 degrees. When the milk has stabilized at 90 degrees add three tablespoons of lactic starter or five tablespoons of buttermilk. Stir the milk vigorously for five minutes.

Twenty minutes after adding the starter prepare to color the milk. Dissolve a color tablet in two tablespoons of cool water and stir it into the milk for five minutes. Stir the milk frequently until the rennet is added.

One hour and ten minutes after adding the starter prepare to add the rennet. Dissolve the rennet in two tablespoons of water and stir into the milk immediately. Stir continuously for five minutes, then stop stirring and remove all of the utensils from the kettle. When the milk has coagulated, in about thirty minutes, cut the curd into one-quarter-inch cubes.

After cutting the curd remove the kettle from the heat and allow the curd to settle to the bottom of the kettle. As the curd settles, carefully remove sixteen ounces of whey. Place the whey into a small saucepan and heat it to 160 degrees. When the whey is hot, gently begin stirring the curd. Slowly pour the hot whey back into the cooking kettle, stirring constantly. Check the temperature after all of the hot whey has been mixed with the curd. The curd should now be approximately 97 degrees. Allow the curd to settle once again and remove sixteen ounces of whey. Reheat the whey to 160 degrees and pour it back into the curd while stirring continuously. Add only enough whey the second time to raise the temperature to 104 degrees. If, after adding the second measure of hot whey, the temperature is still below 103 degrees, prepare a third batch of hot whey and add only enough to raise the temperature to 104 degrees.

Line a colander with muslin and place it into the sink. Pour the curd into the colander and allow it to drain for twenty minutes. After ten minutes press the curd gently, with your hands, to force out the excess whey.

While the curd is draining prepare the cheese press by lining the press with muslin. After the curd has drained for twenty minutes transfer it into the press. Press the curd with moderate pressure for two hours. Then remove the cheese from the press and remove the cloth. Rewrap the cheese in a fresh cloth and return it to the press. Press the cheese for three hours at moderate pressure.

Prepare a brine solution by dissolving canning salt in one quart of 50-degree water until no more salt will dissolve. This will give you a saturated brine solution. Add one cup of cool water to this solution. Place the entire cheese press, with the cheese in it, into the brine. Be sure the cheese is completely covered by the solution to prevent drying. Keep the brine at 50 degrees and let the cheese soak for twenty-four hours. Remove the cheese from the press and let it dry for about two days before sealing it in paraffin. Cure the finished cheese for two to three months at 50 degrees.

7

THE ITALIAN CHEESES

The Italian cheeses are the cheeses I love to eat and the same ones which have nearly led me to beating my head on the oven door. They are difficult to make right, especially in small quantities. Obtaining the stringy, plasticity of a soft Italian cheese is a frustrating process. Just when you feel sure it is getting just the right consistency, the cheese suddenly turns dry and doughy. I once had an entire three-quarter-pound ball of mozzarella dissolve in the hot whey in which it was cooking; this happened only once and I have no idea where the cheese went, but it was definitely gone. I am confessing all of these problems, not to scare you off, but to give you a rough idea of the problems which you may encounter while making *pasta filata* (plastic-curd cheese). I have made very good mozzarella and excellent ricotta, so it is possible but you may have more than a few unfortunate experiences along the way.

PARMESAN CHEESE

Parmesan is a very hard cheese which is usually grated for use in cooking. The cheese will keep almost indefinitely when fully cured. It was first made in the vicinity of Parma, Italy, hence its name. The process for making this cheese is fairly simple but curing it will present some problems.

Before you get started it may be a good idea to look for a place which can be kept at 54 to 60 degrees for about one and one-half years. I would suggest an unused refrigerator set at its warmest temperature. It would also be a good idea to build a small curing chamber (see Appendix 2) in which the humidity can be kept very high. If these two things have not slowed you down you should have no great trouble making Parmesan. You will also need a metal cylinder about six inches in diameter and a circular board that fits inside of the cylinder. The cylinder should be punched full of one-eighth-inch holes. Punch the holes from the inside to the outside of the cylinder.

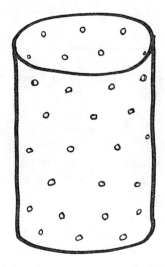

Figure 6. The pressing cylinder for Parmesan cheese.

To punch the holes in the cylinder you can build a simple tool. From a lumberyard, obtain two pieces of two-by-two lumber about one foot long—these pieces may be scrap material and cost you nothing. Pound an eightpenny (2½-inch) nail through one of the boards near the end. Pound the nail all the way in so that the point is sticking about one inch out of the board. Clamp this board securely in a vise, slip the cylinder over the board, and rest it against the point of the nail. Now use the other board to hit the cylinder where it rests on the nail. Wham! a neat hole punched from the inside of the cylinder.

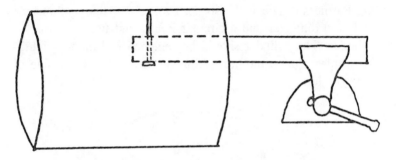

Figure 7. Some simple tools for punching holes in a metal cylinder.

The procedure given is for two gallons of milk but if you can handle a larger quantity it will be worth your while since the curing time is quite long and the yield is about one-half the amount you have been getting from the softer cheeses. Those of you who have not been frightened away can now begin to make Parmesan.

Place two gallons of 2 per cent milk into a kettle and heat it to 96 degrees. When the temperature has stabilized, add a combination starter of *L. bulgaricus* and *S. thermophilus*. Add one-half cup of starter or use three-quarters cup of fresh yogurt. Stir the starter into the milk vigorously for five minutes. Cheese coloring may be added, if you wish, thirty minutes after adding the starter.

One hour and fifteen minutes after adding the starter, rennet should be added to the milk. Dissolve the rennet in one-quarter cup of cool water and stir it into the milk immediately. Stir continuously for five minutes and then remove all of the utensils from the kettle. The milk should be coagulated after about thirty minutes. Be sure to test for proper curd development before cutting the curd.

Cut the curd into one-quarter-inch cubes and begin stirring the curd as soon as the curd is cut. Continue stirring and cutting until the curd particles are uniformly cut into one-eighth to three-sixteenths-inch cubes. After cutting the curd begin heating the curd slowly so that the temperaure is 120 degrees after forty-five minutes. Stir almost continuously during the heating and holding process. Hold the temperature between 120 and 130 degrees until the curd is quite firm.

The curd is firm when it sinks immediately to the bottom of the kettle when stirring is stopped. When you judge the curd to be sufficiently firm, allow it to settle to the bottom of the kettle and rest for ten minutes. Do not apply any heat to the kettle when the curd is resting to prevent it from becoming excessively heated at the bottom. Overcooking, by overheating, can cause uneven curd dryness and afterward uneven curing.

After the curd has rested for ten minutes, pour it into a colander lined with cheesecloth. Gather the curd into the cloth and hang it up to drain for twenty minutes.

Place the press cylinder on a wire screen set on a drain board. Place the bag of drained curd into the cylinder and fold the cloth as neatly as possible over the top of the cheese. Place the circular board on top of the curd and press it down firmly with your hand. Then place a wooden block into the cylinder and add a ten-pound weight on top of the block to provide a constant pressure on the compressed curd. After one hour remove the block and weight, turn the press over, and replace the block and weight to press the cheese from the opposite side. Repeat this process every hour for the next three hours.

After four hours of pressing remove the cheese from the press and remove the cloth from the cheese. Then replace the unwrapped cheese in the press and increase the weight to fifteen to twenty pounds. Allow the cheese to press in this way for eighteen hours; turn the cheese over at least twice during this time. After pressing, remove the block and weight and place the cheese in a room which is constantly 60 to 65 degrees. Leave the cheese in the press and let it stand for three days.

After letting the cheese stand for three days it will be necessary to prepare a salt solution for brining the cheese. The easiest way to do this is to fill a bowl with one-half gallon of water at 60 degrees. This is the temperature at which the brining is done and the solution should be saturated at this temperature. Stir canning salt into the water until the salt will no longer dissolve. Add a pint of fresh water and stir to dissolve any salt in the bottom of the bowl. You now have a saturated salt solution in which to brine your cheese.

Remove the cheese from the press and place it into the brine solution. Keep the bowl covered to prevent evaporation and turn the cheese daily. Soak the cheese in the brine for ten days. After salting, allow the cheese to dry in air for six to eight days. All the salting and drying should be done at 60 degrees.

After drying, place the cheese in a room which is 58 degrees and has a relative humidity of 80 to 85 per cent. The cheese must be kept in this condition for about one year. Here is where a small curing chamber in a spare refrigerator will come in handy. The high humidity can be more easily maintained if the chamber is small. Wash and scrape the cheese to keep it clean and rub it with oil from time to time to lubricate the surface.

After this initial curing period the relative humidity should be increased to 90 per cent and the cheese held in this atmosphere for two months. The cheese should now be fully cured, very hard and rather dry. Parmesan can be easily grated for use in soups, salads, or macaroni.

If the cheese should develop cracks during the curing process, raise the relative humidity 5 per cent and seal the cracks with vegetable shortening. If the cheese becomes slimy the relative humidity is probably too high and should be lowered about 5 per cent; the temperature might also be too high if there is excessive mold growth.

When fully cured the cheese should be very hard with a waxy texture and virtually free of any mold growth. Because of its low moisture content, Parmesan will keep for almost an indefinite time under refrigeration.

ROMANO CHEESE

Romano is probably the most popular of the very hard Italian cheeses. It was originally made from ewe's milk but is now made mostly from cow's milk. In some areas of Southern Italy it is made from goat's milk and called Caprino Romano. Sardo is a Romano-type cheese made in Sardinia.

Romano is most commonly used in the United States as a grated cheese. But when mildly aged it is also an excellent table cheese. The imported cheeses are colored black on the outside and rubbed with olive oil to seal any pores and to improve their appearance.

Making Romano, like Parmesan, should be no great problem but the curing process is over one year in length in order to produce a grating cheese. Romano has a higher fat content and more moisture than Parmesan and because of this it will not keep as long and will develop into a sharper and more piquant cheese than Parmesan. As with Parmesan you will need a curing chamber and a pressing cylinder. The cylinder should be about six inches in diameter and ten inches high. A circular board, which fits loosely inside of the cylinder, will be used to press the curd.

For those of you who are super-serious about making Parmesan and Romano, it takes twenty-five gallons of milk to make a single, full size cheese. The cheese should be ten inches in diameter and about six inches thick. Of course, your press and curing chamber will have to be adjusted in size accordingly.

Romano can be made from unpasteurized milk since it requires at least six months of aging. If you use unpasteurized milk eliminate the starter. It should be kept in mind, however, that if raw milk is used the chance of developing a bad cheese is greatly increased.

Place one gallon of 2 per cent milk plus one gallon of regular homogenized milk into a kettle. Heat the milk to 90 degrees and add one-half cup of a combination starter or three-quarters cup of fresh yogurt. The combination starter should be a mixture of *L. bulgaricus* and *S. thermophilus*. Stir the starter into the milk vigorously for five minutes. Use double the amount of rennet and dissolve it in one-quarter cup of cool, soft water. Stir the rennet into the milk vigorously for three minutes. Then remove all of the utensils and let the milk stand undisturbed for twenty mniutes.

Test the milk for coagulation. After it has set, cut the curd into one-quarter-inch cubes. Allow the curd to rest for ten minutes after cutting and before starting to cook it. Heat the curd very slowly to 118 degrees. The temperature should increase about one degree every three minutes. Stir the curd gently and slowly at first; stir the curd constantly after it has reached 108 degrees. Hold the curd at 118 until it is firm and sinks quickly to the bottom of the kettle when the stirring is stopped. Remove the kettle from the heat and continue stirring for about two minutes. Allow the curd to settle to the bottom of the kettle while you prepare to press the curd.

Line a colander with cheesecloth and place it into the sink. Pour the curd into the colander and let it drain for twenty minutes. Transfer the curd to a large, warm bowl or return it to the cooking kettle for salting. Add salt to the curd and stir it into the curd until it is completely dissolved. Use three teaspoons of salt for each gallon of milk used.

Place your press cylinder on a draining board and cover it with a large piece of cheesecloth. Spoon the curd into the cylinder and fold the cheesecloth neatly over the top of the curd. Place a board on top of the cheese and a ten-pound weight on the board. After one hour remove the weight and board and turn the cheese over. Replace the board and weight and press the cheese for another hour. Repeat this process every hour for the next three hours.

Take the cheese from the press and remove the cheesecloth covering. Replace the cheese in the press and place the board on top of the cheese. Now place a fifteen- to twenty-pound weight on the board and press the cheese for eighteen hours turning it in the press every six to eight hours.

After pressing, brine the cheese for two days. To do this you must prepare a brine solution. Place one-half gallon of water into a large bowl. The water should be cooled to 60 degrees before adding any salt. Stir canning salt into the water until it will no longer dissolve. Add a pint of fresh water to the brine and stir to make sure all of the salt has dissolved. Place the cheese into the brine and cover the bowl with plastic film to prevent evaporation. Keep the brine solution at about 60 degrees throughout the brining process. After twenty-four hours turn the cheese over and re-cover the bowl. Brine the cheese for another twenty-four hours.

Remove the cheese from the brine and place it on a cake cooling rack for drying. Place the rack and cheese into the refrigerator and adjust the temperature to about 60 degrees. The refrigerator you use for curing cheese should not be a self defrosting or frost free type because these are much too dry inside for cheese. A good, old-fashioned, frost-an-inch-thick-in-the-freezer, refrigerator is much better for curing cheese. There won't be any frost in the freezer anyway because you will be keeping it much too warm to have frost; rain, yes; frost, no. Dry the cheese for about four days, turning it daily.

The cheese is now ready to be placed into the curing chamber. Adjust the temperature to 50 degrees and the relative humidity to 85 per cent. Clean the surface of the cheese daily, scraping it if necessary. Turn the cheese over daily, also. Cure the cheese in this way for six months to obtain a table-style Romano. Cure the cheese for a year if you wish to use it for grating. If the cheese begins to crack, increase the relative humidity and seal the cracks with vegetable shortening. If, on the other hand, the cheese turns slimy or moldy, lower the relative humidity and clean off any traces of mold or slimy deposits. The finished cheese should be virtually mold free, hard, and quite sharp to the taste.

CACIOCAVALLO CHEESE

Caciocavallo is an Italian cheese very similar to Provolone. It has somewhat less fat than Provolone and usually is not smoked. Like almost all of the Italian cheeses, I found it difficult to make correctly. The small amount of curd obtained has a definite tendency to overcook and dry out. The cooking times given should, therefore, be used mainly for ref-

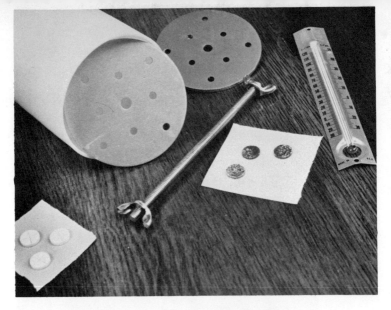

Plate 1. Cheese press with metal plates, plastic sleeve, threaded rod, wing nuts, color tablets (right), and rennet tablets (left).

Plate 2. Testing milk for proper coagulation. Note how the curd breaks smoothly away from the sides of the container.

Plate 3. Curd being cut into ⅜″ cubes.

Plate 4. Partially cooked Cheddar cheese curd.

Plate 5. Cooked curd draining in a colander before matting or pressing.

Plate 6. Curd being matted in the bottom of the cooking kettle.

Plate 7. The curd after the first matting step.

Plate 8. Neufchâtel being pressed between boards. The same method is used whenever pressing between boards is called for.

erence; the actual condition of the curd should determine when the cheese is properly cooked.

Caciocavallo and mozzarella are known as *pasta filata* or plastic-curd cheese. This means that the cheese is smooth, cohesive, and can be stretched to form long threads. Remember the last pizza you had and the long, stringy strands of cheese which tenaciously prevented the pieces from being separated? Producing this plasticity in the cheese is the most difficult process I have encountered in cooking cheese. The method described is the Italian method, which differs somewhat from the American cheese factory method. However, I feel we should be striving for the more authentic method as long as we are going through all the trouble to make cheese in the first place.

Caciocavallo is made from cow's milk, although sometimes a mixture of cow's and ewe's milk is used. Heat one gallon of whole milk to 96 degrees in the cheese cooking assembly. Use milk with between 3 and 3½ per cent of butterfat. When the milk has stabilized at 96 degrees, lactic starter can be added. Add one tablespoon of lactic culture plus one tablespoon of *S. thermophilus* or add two tablespoons of buttermilk plus three tablespoons of yogurt. Stir the starters into the milk thoroughly and let the milk ripen for thirty minutes.

After thirty minutes, rennet should be added to the milk. Dissolve double the amount of rennet usually used for one gallon of milk in one-quarter cup of cool, soft water and stir it into the milk vigorously for five minutes. The milk should be ready to cut in thirty minutes; be sure to test for proper coagulation before cutting the curd.

Cut the curd into pea-size pieces. Stir the curd and continue cutting until no large curds are left. After cutting the curd, allow it to stand until the curd sinks to the bottom of the kettle. When the curd is firmly settled to the bottom, bail off as much whey as possible and save for use later. After removing the whey, compress the curd, with your hands, into a mass which can be removed from the kettle.

The curd is then transferred to a wooden bucket. An insulated ice bucket would be a good substitute for a wooden tub. Heat the whey to 140 to 150 degrees and pour it over the curd. Use only enough whey to cover the cheese and add fresh, hot whey whenever the temperature of the cheese falls below 140 degrees. After some time a vigorous fermentation will begin. Five hours after fermentation begins the curd should be tested for elasticity. Dip a sample of the curd into near boiling water and then stretch it. When the curd can be drawn into a tough, springy fiber it is ready for draining. It may take anywhere from five to twenty hours, after fermentation begins, to develop the proper elasticity.

Remove the cheese from the hot whey and allow it to drain while you heat one-half gallon of water to 175 to 180 degrees. Pour the whey out of the wooden tub or ice bucket. Cut the cheese into two strips and place these into the bucket. Pour the hot water over the strips and work them with a spoon until they are very elastic. Remove one of the strips from the water and form it into a pear shaped mass. Continue dipping the cheese into the hot water to prevent its cooling off and to give it a smooth surface. When the cheese is nicely shaped and very smooth, place it in a bowl of cold water to cool and harden. Repeat the process on the second strip.

Allow the cheese to cool in water for about three hours. Prepare a brine solution of canning salt in 50-degree water. Submerge the cheeses in the brine and hold them at 50 degrees for three days. After brining, the cheeses are cured at 62 degrees and 85 per cent relative humidity for three months. Clean and oil the cheeses whenever they become moldy. If you wish to use the cheese for grating, cure it for six to twelve months. The yield, I might add, is quite low for this type of cheese, so don't be too disappointed when you only get nine ounces of cheese from a gallon of milk.

MOZZARELLA CHEESE, TYPE I

Mozzarella is the pizza cheese. It is a soft, stringy cheese used primarily in cooking. Mozzarella is quite bland-tasting since it contains no salt, but when melted on a pizza or lasagna dish it is a rich and delicious cheese. The finished cheeses average between eight ounces and one pound and can easily be made from a gallon of milk. The cheese is eaten while fresh and for this reason should be made from pasteurized milk. The milk originally used to make mozzarella was buffalo's milk; cow's milk has now largely replaced buffalo's milk, especially in the United States where buffalos simply are not kept as livestock. If you happen to have access to a buffalo, however, the procedure is the same as for cow's milk.

Place one gallon of whole, pasteurized milk into a kettle and heat it to 90 degrees. When the temperature has stabilized, add both a lactic starter and a combination starter. Stir two tablespoons of lactic starter and two tablespoons of a combination of *L. bulgaricus* and *S. thermophilus* into the milk for about five minutes. If you prefer, you may substitute four tablespoons of buttermilk and three tablespoons of yogurt for starters.

Dissolve the rennet in two tablespoons of cool water and immediately add it to the milk. Stir vigorously for three minutes; remove all of the utensils from the kettle and allow the milk to stand undisturbed until it has coagulated.

Test the milk for coagulation about forty-eight minutes after adding the rennet. If the curd has coagulated within the first thirty minutes decrease the amount used in future batches.

Cut the curd into one-inch cubes and let it stand for ten minutes.

Prepare a large, double-layer of cheesecloth and place it into a colander. Spoon the curd from the kettle to the colander with a slotted spoon for draining. After all of the curd is in the colander gather the corners of the cheesecloth together and hang the cloth bag and curd over a sink. Allow the curd to drain for thirty minutes.

Up to this point you should have had no problems. From this point on, however, a good deal of experimentation will be necessary before a good technique can be developed. Kneading and stretching the curd is an important and difficult procedure. Elasticity developes as the cooking and kneading progress; unfortunately, the stringy and elastic cheese you are cooking can suddenly turn into a dry and crumbly mass. Knowing when to move on to the next step is strictly a matter of experience, or maybe, luck.

Heat about one-half gallon of water to 120 degrees. Place the drained curd into a warm kettle and pour enough of the heated water over the curd to cover it. Add hot water as needed to maintain a temperature of 116 degrees. Knead and stretch the curd until it can be formed into a stretchy mass. This step should be done slowly and should take about forty to fifty minutes.

Bail some of the water from the kettle and replace it with the hottest tap water available. Avoid heating the kettle directly to prevent overcooking near the bottom of the kettle. Slowly raise the temperature to 135 degrees. Continue kneading and stretching the curd in the hot water until it becomes smooth and cohesive. The cheese should become very much like a sticky bread dough and form long strips when stretched.

Flatten the curd until it is about a one-inch-thick pancake. Let the curd rest in the hot water while you heat a quart of water to 190 degrees. When the water is hot transfer the cheese to a clean kettle and pour the very hot water over it until it is submerged. Work the cheese with a wooden spoon until it becomes rubbery. Fold the cheese in half and then in half again to form a triangle. Remove the cheese from the water and form it by hand into a ball. Dip the cheese in the hot water to keep the surface smooth and glossy. When the cheese has been neatly formed, dunk it into a pan of cold water and allow it to cool for several hours. Mozzarella is eaten fresh and is ready for use as soon as it is cool.

MOZZARELLA CHEESE, TYPE II

It is probably a lie to call this cheese mozzarella; for that matter, this cheese may not have a name at all and should be known only as Italian-style cheese, whatever that means. The method has the advantage of being very easy and since it has no real name it cannot be compared to anything and, therefore, you simply cannot make a bad one, whatever it is. It is cheese though, and edible, and you may even like it.

Heat one gallon of milk to 96 degrees and add four tablespoons of buttermilk plus three tablespoons of yogurt. If you prefer you may substitute a combination starter of *L. bulgaricus* and *S. thermophilus*. Stir the starters into the milk vigorously for about five minutes. Thirty minutes after adding the starters prepare to add the rennet.

Dissolve the rennet in two tablespoons of cool water and stir immediately into the milk. Stir continuously for three minutes, then remove all of the utensils and allow the milk to coagulate.

Test the milk for coagulation. Begin heating the curd very slowly and at the same time break up the curd with your hands. This procedure can be a very sensuous thing which will either turn you on or make you wish you were washing the walls. Dipping one's hands into a very soft gelatin, which is at body temperature, almost always has a definite effect on a person. Work the curd with your hands and continue heating it until it is as hot as your hands can tolerate. The whey should be about 135 degrees. If it is much cooler, continue stirring the whey until it is 135 degrees.

Gather the curd together with your hands and form it into a large ball. Assemble the cheese press, the one with the wing nuts and threaded rod, and line it with cheesecloth. Place the ball of curd into the press and fold the cheesecloth over the end. Place the second end plate and wing nut on the rod and turn the wing nuts down by hand until they are tight.

Place the cheese, press and all, into the warm whey and begin heating it. Heat the whey to 200 degrees, then remove the kettle from the heat, cover it, and let it stand until it is cool. Remove the press from the whey and let it drain on its side for twenty-four hours. Remove the cheese from the press and there it is; Italian-style cheese.

RICOTTA CHEESE (WHEY CHEESE)

This is the cheese designed especially for those of you who were sure something could be done with all that whey that has been dumped down the drain. It is also the cheese for making real lasagna. Ricotta is cheese that is made from whey and is mostly coagulated albumin. It is called an Italian cheese because it was first made in Italy but it is not exclusively Italian for it is made throughout Europe and in Wisconsin and New York in the United States. Ricotta is known by as many different names as there are countries which make it.

Ricotta is made from the sweet whey obtained from Cheddar, Colby, Swiss, Provolone, or mozzarella. In addition, it is necessary to have an acid coagulant such as the whey from small curd cottage cheese. The sweet whey must be as fresh as possible so that a minimum of acid is formed and heating is begun immediately after it is drained from the curd. The sour whey should be warm and reasonably fresh.

Ricotta is normally an uncolored cheese and if you wish it to be uncolored it must be made from the whey of an uncolored cheese. Colored ricotta has exactly the same flavor as the uncolored variety, however, so it is merely a matter of aesthetics.

As soon as the whey is drained from the curd begin heating it quite rapidly. If fresh, moist ricotta is the desired end product, add ten ounces of whole milk to the whey; if dry ricotta is to be made, add ten ounces of skim milk to the whey. Heat the whey to 200 degrees. Warm about one quart of sour whey to 110 degrees and line a small wire strainer with cheesecloth.

Pour about one cup of the sour whey into the hot, sweet whey and stir it in. In a few seconds a curd-like material will float to the surface. This is ricotta. Use a tea strainer to skim off the ricotta and dump it into the cheesecloth for draining. When all of the cheese has been skimmed off, add another cup of sour whey and repeat the process. Repeat this procedure until no more ricotta comes to the surface when the sour whey is added. The hot whey can now be discarded.

Allow the cheese to drain and cool to 100 degrees. Transfer the curd to a bowl and stir in one teaspoon of lactic starter and one and one-half teaspoons of salt. If lactic starter is not available it can be omitted but it is desirable for improving flavor. The cheese should then be pressed moderately for three hours for moist ricotta and more firmly for six hours if dry ricotta is made. The cheese should be kept at 100 degrees while pressing and drying. After pressing, the cheese should be dried in warm air for several hours. Wrap it in foil or plastic film and store it in the refrigerator.

8

SWISS CHEESE

Swiss, or Emmenthaler, is known as the King of Cheeses. I have no idea why it is called that although I am sure there are many who feel it is quite proper. It is, without a doubt, one of the most difficult cheeses to make. Swiss originally come from Switzerland (I'll bet you are surprised to hear that) and more precisely from the Emmenthal Valley, which is why Swiss is called Emmenthaler. Its history dates back to the mid 1400s and it was exported almost from the start. Swiss is a large, hard cheese with a mildly sweet, nutlike flavor and is full of holes. It is these holes which give Swiss its distinctive flavor, not the holes really but the bacteria which produce the holes also produce the flavor.

Swiss cheese requires the presence of three species of bacteria. The first two are no problem, they are *S. thermophilus* and *L. bulgaricus*. The last is a bit more difficult to find; *Propionibacterium shermanii* or propionic acid-forming bacteria. It is the propionic acid-forming process which causes the eyes and the flavor. Award-winning Swiss cheeses are made by factories who guard their methods and recipes like trade secrets. The time of the year, the rainfall, the kind of cows, and many other variables affect the quality of the cheese. The best cheese is made from raw milk taken from certified cows. The milk is standardized and often clarified before manufacturing is begun.

To make Swiss you will need a few tools. First, a flat wire whisk; that is the fan-shaped wire thing with the handle you have seen in kitchens and have wondered what to use it for.

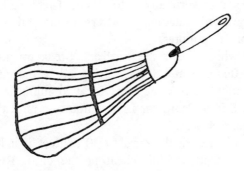

Figure 8. A wire whisk.

Second, you will need a gallon can with smooth sides for a mold. Punch about five or six dozen small holes into this can from the *inside* out. And lastly, you will need a cake cooling rack. In addition to these tools a combination culture of *S. thermophilus* and *L. bulgaricus* and a culture of *Propionibacterium shermanii* must be prepared. If you do not wish to make cultures you can use yogurt as a starter, however, there will be no holes in your cheese and it will lack flavor.

Place one and one-half gallons of fresh milk into a kettle and allow it to come to room temperature. Stir in one tablespoon of combination culture and one teaspoon of propionic acid culture. You can substitute one tablespoon of yogurt for the starters. Let the milk stand for thirty minutes.

Remove one quart of milk from the kettle and set it aside. Heat the milk in the kettle to 110 degrees stirring constantly with a spoon. After ten minutes, add the quart of cooler milk and allow the whole mixture to stabilize at 90 degrees.

Dissolve the rennet in two tablespoons of cool water and stir it into the milk vigorously for three minutes. Remove all of the utensils and allow the milk to coagulate. Test for coagulation after twenty-five minutes.

Cut the curd vertically into one-half-inch columns. Do not cut the curd diagonally. After cutting, allow the curd to stand for five minutes.

Use the whisk to stir the curd and break up the columns of curd. After one minute of stirring allow the curd to rest for three minutes. Stir the curd for two minutes and let it rest again. Stir the curd for four minutes or until the curd is about the size of peas.

Very slowly reheat the curd to 90 degrees if it has cooled off. Stir constantly while reheating the curd. Remove the kettle from the heat and stir gently for ten minutes.

Place the perforated mold on a drain board and, with a slotted spoon, transfer the curd to the mold. Fill the mold carefully to prevent any open areas inside of the cheese. Tamp down the curd to settle it in the mold and smooth out the surface with a spoon.

Set the cheese stand at room temperature for twenty-four hours turning it over every six hours. After twenty-four hours the cheese should be firm enough to stand without the mold. Carefully remove the mold and transfer the cheese to the cake cooling rack.

Sprinkle about one teaspoon of salt over the top surface and allow the salt to dissolve. When it has dissolved, rub the salt very gently into the top and sides of the cheese. Place the cheese in the curing chamber and hold it at 58 degrees for twenty-four hours. Remove the cheese from the curing chamber and turn it over. Sprinkle the top of the cheese with salt and rub the dissolved salt into the top and sides.

Place the cheese onto the curing chamber and hold it at 55 degrees and 85 per cent relative humidity for three to five weeks. After the first three days turn the cheese daily. After turning the cheese wash the surface very lightly with salt water and clean the rack in the curing chamber to prevent unnecessary mold growth. Do not rub the cheese while washing it but try to bathe it lightly with the salty water.

After about three weeks a white rind will develop. As the cheese continues to age this rind will take on a pinkish hue. When the rind develops this pink color the cheese is ready to eat. If the rind fails to develop, the curing temperature may be too low. Raise the temperature to 60 degrees and allow a few more weeks to pass.

Following the procedure just given will yield about one pound of Swiss cheese. However, if you wish to make a more substantial amount of cheese, the factory method can be followed. There are several differences between the two methods and you may wonder if the procedures are both for Swiss cheese. The end products bear the same name and the variations are caused primarily by the difference in the quantity of curd. I would not recommend using the factory method with less than ten gallons of milk, however.

Heat the milk to 90 degrees and add one tablespoon of combination starter per gallon. Fresh yogurt can be substituted for the combination starter. Also add one teaspoon of propionic acid culture for each gallon of milk. Stir the starters into the milk constantly for ten minutes.

Dissolve enough rennet for the quantity of milk you are using in two ounces of water for each gallon of milk. In other words, dissolve the rennet for ten gallons of milk in twenty ounces of water. The amount of rennet should be sufficient to permit cutting the curd in thirty minutes. If the milk does not coagulate in thirty minutes increase the amount of rennet in future batches. Stir the rennet into the milk vigorously for six to eight minutes, then remove the utensils and allow the milk to coagulate.

Cut the curd, vertically only, into one-inch-square columns. Use your hands or a large scoop and turn the curd upside down in the kettle. The objective of this is to get the creamier milk near the surface moved to the bottom of the kettle so that the cheese will be more uniform. If you are using homogenized milk this step may be omitted. After turning the curd over, cut it into one-inch cubes. Let the curd rest for five minutes then use a large wire whisk to stir and cut the curd into one-eighth-inch particles. The final cutting is done slowly and should take ten to fifteen minutes.

The temperature should be held at 88 to 94 degrees throughout the cutting process and for the next thirty minutes. The curd should develop a firmness similar to that of cottage cheese during this time. If it has not firmed up after thirty minutes the curd should be held at the same temperature until it becomes firm. The curd should be stirred gently but frequently during the firming-up period.

As soon as the curd is sufficiently firm begin heating the curd. Apply enough heat to raise the temperature to 122 degrees in thirty minutes. Stir continuously while heating the curd to prevent the curd from sticking or matting. Hold the curd at 122 until the curd particles can be easily separated after being squeezed together in your hand. When this condition is reached the cooking should be stopped and the curd allowed to settle to the bottom of the kettle. Remove about one third of the whey after the curd has settled.

Dip the curd from the kettle and place it into a coarse cloth sack for draining. Drain the curd for about two hours and then place the sack and the curd into a mold. Smooth out the cloth as much as possible in the mold before pressing the cheese. The mold should be about ten inches high and large enough in diameter to accommodate all of the curd. The mold should also be perforated to allow the whey to drain and should be placed on a board for draining. A board somewhat smaller than the mold should be placed on the curd and about twenty pounds of weight placed on the board to press the cheese.

Turn the cheese over and replace the pressing board after one hour of pressing. Repeat this process every six hours for the next twenty-four hours.

Remove the cheese from the mold and very carefully remove the cloth. Place the cheese into a brine solution for two days. Sprinkle salt on the exposed surface. The brining should be carried out at 55 degrees and 85 per cent relative humidity. After twenty-four hours turn the cheese over and salt the newly exposed surface.

After brining, place the cheese into a curing chamber until a good rind has developed (five to ten days). The curing chamber should be held at 55 degrees and 85 per cent relative humidity. Wash the cheese daily with a weak salt solution, turn it over and sprinkle the surface lightly with salt. When a suitable rind has developed, the cheese is ripened at a higher temperature.

Clean the curing chamber thoroughly and then place the cheese into it for final ripening. The temperature should be about 70 degrees and the relative humidity about 80 per cent. Turn the cheese every two days. Wash the cheese with salt water and rub the surface gently with dry salt. The cheese is ripened for about four to six weeks, then placed into storage at 40 degrees. The cheese is ready to eat four months after making it. Cheese imported from Switzerland usually is six to ten months old, so you may wish to increase your aging time to gain the imported flavor.

9

CAMEMBERT CHEESE

Camembert will be the ultimate challenge to the amateur cheese maker. The making process is not particularly difficult but successfully curing a Camembert can be justly compared to winning the decathlon. The skill required is tremendous and a large measure of perseverance certainly can do no harm. Simply determining when the Camembert is properly cured contains an element of risk; if it is cut too soon, the curing process will be upset and will no longer proceed normally. If you wait too long, the cheese becomes overripe and loses quality rapidly. But take heart, you may have a special hidden talent and produce a good Camembert the first time around.

Start by preparing two two-pound coffee cans for molding Camembert. Cut both the top and bottom from each can. Then punch about three dozen nail holes into each can distributing them evenly over the sides; punch the holes from the *inside to the outside of the can*. It will also be a good idea to have a curing chamber since Camembert is a mold-ripened cheese (see Appendix 2).

The next step, believe it or not, is to buy a Camembert that you especially like. Do not eat this Camembert yet, you will need it for the mold spores which it contains. This piece of prepared Camembert will provide the mold necessary to ripen the cheese you are about to make.

Cut a one-inch square of cheese from just below the rind. Cut it about one-quarter-inch thick and mash and dissolve it in a half pint of sterile water at about 80 to 85 degrees. Strain this solution through a fine cheesecloth and save the liquid to inoculate the milk. Heat five quarts of whole milk to 90 degrees and add six tablespoons of lactic culture or three-quarters cup of fresh buttermilk. Pour in the water containing the dissolved cheese and stir slowly for ten minutes. Allow the milk to ripen for a total of fifty minutes, stirring occasionally. After fifty minutes prepare to add rennet to the milk.

Dissolve the rennet in one-quarter cup of cool, soft water and stir it into the milk immediately. Stir the milk vigorously for five minutes, then remove the utensils and allow the milk to coagulate. Test the milk for coagulation forty-five minutes after adding the rennet. If the milk is not firmly set, allow it to stand another one-half hour and test it again. The curd should be kept at 90 degrees until ready for molding and the room temperature should be no more than 70 degrees. Too warm a room will adversely affect the initial curing process.

Obtain four woven reed or nylon mats which are somewhat larger than the molds you have made. Woven place mats should work very well for this purpose. Reed mats should be unfinished and uncolored. Wash the mats thoroughly and place two of them on a drain board. Place the drain board in a sink so that the whey, which will drain through the mats, can run off and be disposed of without making a mess on the counter. Place one mold on each mat and ladle half of the curd into each mold using a slotted spoon.

Let the curd drain at room temperature for at least three

hours or until it is firm enough to be turned. Place a flat metal plate, such as the bottom of a layer cake pan, on top of the mold. Slide your hand under the mat to support the curd and quickly invert the whole assembly. Rinse the mat thoroughly and replace it on the drain board. Place the mold and the metal plate on the mat and then carefully draw out the metal plate leaving the curd once again resting on the mat. The top side of the curd should show the imprint of the mat clearly on its surface. If the curd was turned too soon the impression will quickly disappear from the wet curd. If the curd is draining too slowly to meet this schedule it should probably be eaten fresh since it will not age properly. Repeat the turning process with the second mold and let both drain for another two hours. After two hours turn the molds over again following the same procedure as before. Turn the molds every thirty minutes until the molds have been turned a total of six times.

Place fresh, clean mats on the drain board and then transfer the molds and curd to the fresh mats. Use a knife to loosen the edges of the curd from the molds and remove the molds. Standing before you are now two unripened Camemberts in all of their fragile beauty. Let them stand for five to six hours at 70 to 72 degrees, completely undisturbed. After six hours the cheeses should be firm enough to be handled.

Half fill a shallow pan with canning salt and place the fresh cheese into it. Thoroughly cover the entire cheese with the salt and then return the salted cheese to the draining mat, shaking off any loose salt. The cheeses can now be left to stand overnight at a room temperature no higher than 70. About 67 degrees would be ideal. Right about now I can imagine you saying to yourself that unless the kitchen is air-conditioned no one will be making this stuff in summer. You are exactly right, Camembert is generally made from fall till spring.

The next morning place the cheeses into your curing chamber and adjust the relative humidity to about 90 per cent. The chamber should be placed in the refrigerator and held at 50 to 55 degrees. Leave the cheeses undisturbed for about five days or until white stalks of mold appear on the surface. This mold is *Penicillium camemberti* and is the ripening mold for Camembert cheese. As soon as the mold appears on the surface the cheeses can be turned for the first time.

After the mold has spread uniformly over the surface the relative humidity should be lowered to about 80 per cent. The mold should develope a blue-gray color after about two weeks. If the cheeses start to crack increase the relative humidity and if the cheeses get slimy or turn green or black, lower the relative humidity. Cut off any green or black mold which might appear with a knife. After the blue-gray color has been obtained lower the temperature to 45 to 50 degrees and keep the relative humidity at about 85 per cent. After two or three weeks the mold should turn a reddish color and the cheese feel somewhat sticky to the touch. The cheese is now ready to be eaten and further curing will cause the cheese to liquefy and develop strong flavors.

After curing several batches of cheese it will no longer be necessary to inoculate the milk with the dissolved cheese and water solution because the *P. camemberti* spores will be well-established in the curing chamber. Preserve these spores by keeping the curing chamber in the refrigerator continuously. When a fresh cheese is then placed into the chamber the spores will almost immediately begin growing on its surface. In this way, Camembert of consistent flavor can be produced since the mold will always be of the same strain.

If all has gone well and you have produced a delicately flavored Camembert feel free to heap praise on your skill as a cheese maker. Camembert is probably the most difficult cheese to cure properly and a good cheese is worthy of recognition.

10

BLUE CHEESES

The blue cheeses derive their name from the blue-green *Penicillium roqueforti* mold that grows in veins through the cheese. There are several French, English and Italian cheeses which are classed as blue cheeses; Stilton, Roquefort, Gex, Gorgonzola, Blue Wensleydale, St. Flour, Laguiole, and Mont Cenis are some of the cheeses which contain blue mold. I believe that liking blue cheese is an acquired taste; a taste, I might add, which I have never developed.

Making blue cheese requires a curing chamber and a frame for molding. But more important than these, a blue cheese requires a great deal of time and patience. Conditions inside of the cheese must be right and four to six months of aging is necessary to have a good mold growth.

Penicillium roqueforti is the mold required to make blue cheese. It can be purchased as a powder (see Appendix 1) or you can try to use a piece of blue cheese to inoculate your cheese. Select a piece of blue cheese with good flavor and a large amount of blue mold. Place one-quarter slice of whole wheat bread in a shallow bowl and pour three tablespoons of water over the bread. Then shave the mold off of the cheese and onto the bread and into the water in the bowl. Be generous with the cheese to insure a rapid growth. Cover the bowl loosely with plastic film and let it stand in a cool room until the bread is thoroughly coated with mold. Be certain there is always some water in the bowl because the mold requires a very high humidity for proper growth. The day before you make your cheese remove the bread from the dish and allow it to dry in air until it can be crushed into a powder. When the time comes to add the mold to your curd, crush the bread into a fine powder and sprinkle it over the curd. I think that I should mention that trying to produce your own blue mold powder is a highly unreliable process and you will probably be better off buying the prepared spores.

I have three variations of blue cheese which are more or less suitable for homemaking. The first is similar to English Stilton cheese. The second is a domestic factory version known only as blue cheese. The third is probably the easiest to make and is remotely similar to the French Gex cheese.

STILTON-STYLE CHEESE

Heat three gallons of fresh, whole milk to 84 degrees and stir in three tablespoons of lactic starter or five tablespoons of buttermilk. Stir in the starter for about three minutes.

Use only one-third to one-half the amount of rennet normally used. The time required for the milk to coagulate must be sixty to ninety minutes, and the amount of rennet should be adjusted to obtain this time. Dissolve the rennet in one-half cup of cool water and stir it into the milk vigorously for five minutes. The rennet is added as soon as the starters are added since a minimum of acid must be present when the curd is finally cut. Test the curd for proper coagulation before proceding.

Use a large serving spoon, an unslotted spoon in this case, and cut thin spoonfuls from the curd. Place the curd into a three-foot-square cotton or muslin dish towel placed in a pan. This towel should not be the turkish towel variety but the inexpensive, flat cotton type. When all of the curd is in the towel tie the four corners together to form a tight sack around the curd. Let the sack soak in the draining whey for one-half hour then hang the sack of curd over a sink for further draining.

Drain the curd for about twelve hours. Retie the cloth tightly around the curd every hour to keep the curd draining. After twelve hours the curd should be completely matted into a single mass free of any loose particles or cracks. If it is not, retie the cloth, place a board on the curd and place a pan of water on the board. Press the cheese in this way for one hour and check it again.

When the curd is fully matted it is ready to be cut. Cut the curd into approximately three-inch cubes. These cubes should be firm enough to stand by themselves. Allow the cubes to stand overnight in a cool room, about 60 degrees.

The next morning the cheese is ready for salting and molding. The cheese should be flaky when broken and very acid to the taste. Break the cubes into one and one-half-inch chunks and place them into a bowl. Sprinkle two table-spoons of salt over the curd and stir it in until it is all dissolved.

A mold about the size of a three-pound coffee can should be large enough to hold all of the curd. The mold should be perforated from the inside out to facilitate draining and air flow. If the mold is not tall enough to hold all of the curd, another can of the same size can be cut lengthwise to provide an extension. Compress this can slightly and slip it

into the perforated can to act as an extension. The can used
for the extension should not be perforated. Place the mold
on a board which has been covered with a clean cotton dish
towel.

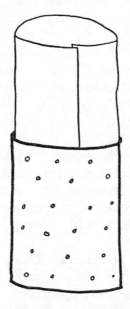

Figure 9. The Stilton cheese press with its extension.

Place a two-inch layer of curd into the mold and press it
down firmly. Sprinkle a *light* dusting of the blue mold powder
over this layer. The powder should be in irregular stripes
rather than an even dusting and should not be closer than
one-half inch from the sides of the mold. Add another layer
of curd but do not press it down. Sprinkle a small amount
of mold powder on this layer. Continue adding layers of
curd until it is used up. Do not put any mold powder on
the last layer. Press the entire mass down lightly with your
hand. Turn the entire mold and cheese over after about four

hours of draining. Use a fresh cloth every time the cheese is turned and wash out the used towel before the next turning so that it can be reused.

Allow the filled mold to stand at 65 degrees for about one week. Turn the cheese once a day. After five days the curd should have settled quite a bit and become somewhat slippery. After seven or more days the curd should be settled down into the mold and have pulled away from the sides of the mold so that it can be easily removed from the mold. If the cheese is not settling quickly enough, poke several holes into the side of the cheese by pushing a wire skewer through the holes in the mold. Salt the top and bottom of the cheese lightly to encourage more draining.

When the cheese is firm enough to stand by itself without spreading out, the mold is removed and the cheese is lightly scraped with a knife to smooth out the surface. After it is scraped the cheese should be wrapped with several layers of cheesecloth. The cloth should be smooth but not excessively tight.

The cheese should be cured at 60 degrees and about 90 per cent relative humidity. The cheesecloth should be changed several times during the next fifteen days. After about fifteen days a white mold should have formed on the surface of the cheese. Remove the cheesecloth so that the mold can spread over the entire surface of the cheese. Keep the cheese in the curing chamber and turn it every day. Clean the rack on which it is standing every time the cheese is turned. The cheese should be ready after four to six months of curing.

If the cheese begins to crack and the humidity is high enough it may be that the temperature is too high for the cheese. Lower the temperature 5 degrees and smooth over the cracked area so that it will heal. To get better blue mold growth skewer the cheese after one month of curing. Do this by running a one-eighth-inch wire halfway through the cheese at about thirty different places. Once the blue mold has developed, you should have a cheese very much like the English Stilton cheese.

FACTORY BLUE-STYLE CHEESE

Factory blue could be the title of a record album but it really is a Roquefort-type cheese commonly made in the United States. For this cheese you will need a metal mold about seven inches in diameter and six inches high and blue mold powder. The procedure given will yield one cheese from three gallons of milk.

Place three gallons of whole, pasteurized, homogenized milk into a kettle and heat it to 84 degrees. Stir one-third cup of lactic starter or two-thirds cup of buttermilk into the milk for five minutes. Dissolve only enough rennet to set the milk in one and a quarter hours. This will be approximately one third to one half the normal amount of rennet. Stir the rennet into the milk for five minutes, remove the utensils, and let the milk coagulate.

When the milk has coagulated, cut the curd into one-half-inch cubes. Let the cut curd stand for ten minutes, then spoon it into a dish towel with a slotted spoon for draining. Tie the corners of the towel together and let it drain for about one hour.

Place the mold on a drain board which has been covered with a clean cloth. Use a large serving spoon to spoon large slabs of curd into the mold. When the entire bottom of the mold has been covered sprinkle it lightly with blue mold powder. Fill the mold one layer at a time and add a small amount of blue mold powder to each layer. Do not, however, place any mold powder on the top layer. The blue mold is to grow inside of the cheese only and should not appear on the surface.

Turn the mold over onto a fresh cloth and board every three hours. Turn the mold over at least six times during the next twenty-four hours, allowing it to rest overnight. The cheese should be firm enough to be handled after twenty-four hours of draining, if it is not it should be left in the mold until it is firm enough to stand alone without spreading. Continue turning the cheese frequently until it can safely be removed from the mold.

After removing it from the mold, allow the cheese to dry for several hours at room temperature. Rub the top and sides of the cheese with coarse canning salt and let the cheese stand until the salt has dissolved. Turn the cheese over and rub salt over the untreated end and the sides. Place the cheese into a curing chamber at 48 degrees and 95 per cent relative humidity. After twenty-four hours remove the cheese, turn it over, and salt the side and top of the cheese again. Return the cheese to the curing chamber. Repeat this process every day for eight days.

After salting the cheese it must be skewered to allow air to enter the cheese. The growth of blue mold requires fresh air to be present. Use a piece of one-eighth-inch wire and pierce the top and bottom of the cheese with about forty holes. If possible the cheese should be kept on its side while it cures. If it does not fit into the curing chamber on its side be certain that there is a free flow of air through the rack to the cheese and turn it over at least once a week. If the cheese is being cured on its side be certain to turn the cheese periodically to prevent flat spots.

Cure the cheese for three months at 48 degrees and 95 per cent relative humidity. Scrape the cheese every three or four weeks to control slime and mold growth. After three months scrape the cheese and wrap it in foil. Store the cheese at 40 degrees in the curing chamber for an additional two or three months. The cheese should now be fully cured and ready to eat.

GEX-STYLE CHEESE

This cheese almost requires that you own your own cow. Not that it requires a lot of milk but the milk must be absolutely fresh. Fresh! like directly from the cow and still warm.

Place the warm milk into a kettle and add enough rennet to cause coagulation in no less than one and one-half hours. Cut the curd into three-quarter-inch chunks and then stir the curd until it is almost liquid. Allow the curd to settle to the bottom of the kettle. After the curd has settled, allow it to stand an additional ten minutes.

Carefully remove as much whey as possible from the kettle, gently stir salt into the curd. Use three teaspoons of salt for each gallon of milk used.

The same mold used for Factory blue may be used for this cheese. In addition to the mold you will need a three-quarter-inch thick pressing board which will fit inside of the mold. Place the mold on a drain board covered with a cloth. Spoon the curd gently into the mold and let it drain for an hour. After one hour turn the mold over and place the pressing board on top of the cheese. Turn the cheese every six hours during the next twenty-four hours.

After twenty-four hours the pressing board and mold can be removed. Rub the entire surface of the cheese generously with coarse canning salt. After salting, sprinkle a small amount of blue mold powder on the top and bottom surfaces of the cheese. Place the cheese into the curing chamber and cure it for four months at 48 degrees and 90 to 95 per cent relative humidity. The blue mold should eventually give the cheese an over-all bluish appearance but none of the mold should be inside of the cheese. In this case, the mold is to grow only on the outside of the cheese. The cheese is ready to eat after four months of curing.

11

YOGURT

Yogurt is not a cheese but it is a popular dairy product that can easily be made at home. Yogurt was rediscovered around the turn of the century but was ignored until recently by all but a few food faddists. People have finally realized that something which is good for them can taste good too.

Yogurt is part skim milk which is fermented with *Streptococcus thermophilus* and *Lactobacillus bulgaricus*. These same organisms are used to make several cheeses and so yogurt is a handy material to have available. The preparation of yogurt for table consumption can be much more varied than yogurt for use as a starter. The flavor can be changed by modifying the ripening time and the incubating temperature. Fruits and flavorings can be added to give yogurt a dessert appeal. Best of all, yogurt is low in calories but very high in nutritional value because of its high milk solids content.

The milk used to make yogurt will also affect the end result. Two per cent part skim milk is usually used to keep calories to a minimum but regular whole milk can be used to give a creamier taste. To improve the body of the yogurt, non-fat dry milk or condensed *skim* milk is added to the fresh milk. The addition of dry milk further increases the milk solids content and greatly improves yogurt's nutritional value.

Yogurt is best prepared about one quart at a time and stored in small-portion-size packages. Four-ounce custard cups are excellent yogurt containers and the small containers allow you to make several flavors at one time.

To make yogurt you must buy either a container of prepared yogurt or a package of dried yogurt culture. The best results will be had if you start with the freeze-dried culture. These cultures are available at all health food stores and many supermarkets carry the cultures in their organic foods departments. Be sure to buy yogurt culture *not* acidophilus culture. Acidophilus milk is an organic preparation which is very useful to persons who are having certain types of intestinal disorders but it is not very palatable and is not a substitute for yogurt.

Milk for the preparation of yogurt must be heat treated to prevent the growth of heat resistant contaminants while incubating the yogurt. Place one-quarter to one-third cup of non-fat dry milk into a sauce pan and add one quart of 2 per cent part skim milk. Stir vigorously to dissolve the dry milk. Instead of dry milk you can substitute eight ounces of condensed *skim* milk to which is added twenty-four ounces of 2 per cent milk.

Heat the milk to 195 degrees and hold the temperature for one hour. Stir frequently to prevent scorching the milk. After one hour remove the milk from the heat and allow it to cool to 104.

While the milk is cooling prepare the containers you plan to use for incubating the yogurt. Custard cups, plastic cups, juice glasses, or just about any small, nonporous containers can be used for yogurt. You will also need a two-inch-deep cake pan to use as a water bath. Eight custard cups will fit into two eight-inch square pans. Heat about one quart of water to 104 degrees to use in the water bath.

When the milk has cooled to 104 degrees stir four *teaspoons* of prepared yogurt or one gram of freeze-dried culture into the milk. Stir for three minutes and then fill each of the custard cups.

Place the cups into the cake pans and add the warm water around the cups. Fill the pan so that the water is the same depth as the milk in the cups. Maintain a temperature of 104 to 113 degrees for six hours and do not stir or disturb the incubating yogurt. The higher temperature will produce a higher acid content and a more sour yogurt. The lower temperature will make a milder yogurt. After incubating the yogurt place it in the refrigerator and store it at 40 degrees. Do not agitate or stir yogurt except to add flavorings since this will cause it to whey off just as cutting cheese curd releases the whey.

The incubation time for yogurt can also be varied. Incubating for three hours will further decrease the acid content and yield a milder flavor. If the yogurt does not coagulate, however, you know that you have gone below the minimum incubating time and will have to increase it for this and future batches.

Always prepare one container of unflavored yogurt for use as starter for the next batch. The yogurt you make can be used to make more yogurt until the results become unsatisfactory. Eventually the yogurt will lose flavor or it will not coagulate and a fresh supply must be made using a culture or a prepared yogurt.

Flavored yogurt can be prepared in two ways. The first is to stir the flavoring into the yogurt just before serving. The second is to incubate the yogurt with the flavoring already added. The second method can be used only with fruits which have been prepared *without* preservatives. The preservatives in canned fruit, particularly sodium benzoate and sorbic acid, will inhibit the growth of the organisms in yogurt. Place the fruit in the bottom of the cup and pour the freshly inoculated milk over the fruit. Most fruits will not affect the incubation time. If you can or freeze your own fruits the second method will produce an excellent yogurt which will not tend to separate as will the yogurt which has been stirred up.

Some of the flavorings added to yogurt are vanilla, chocolate, orange, lemon, strawberry, pineapple, apricot, prune, or even coffee. Just about anything you have a taste for can be added to yogurt. Coffee flavor can be had by placing instant coffee in the cup before pouring in the inoculated milk. Of course, plain yogurt also has an excellent flavor; especially yogurt which has been freshly prepared.

12

RECIPES FOR USING THE
CHEESE YOU HAVE MADE

This section is far from a complete cookbook of cheese recipes but rather it is an accumulation of the very best recipes using cheese that I have found. Any cookbook will tell you how to make macaroni and cheese or a grilled cheese sandwich but a continental cheese pizza or a Stilton fondue are not so easily found. On the other hand, you may have a Camembert that is not quite good enough to eat but would make an excellent Camembert croquette or deep fried Camembert ball if you had a recipe for one. Well, now you do. I have tried to find recipes for using every type of cheese detailed in this book and some of them may seem quite bizzare but I can assure you that they are all quite good. Without further ado, let us start.

APPETIZERS

Blue Cheese Dip

4 ounces blue cheese   *2 tablespoons milk*
3 ounces cream cheese,   *2 tablespoons mayonnaise*
softened

Crumble the blue cheese into a mixing bowl, add the remaining ingredients and beat with an electric mixer until smooth and fluffy. Use celery, tomato wedges, or cucumber slices as dippers. Makes about 1¼ cups of dip.

Blue Cheese Balls

8 ounces cream cheese   *1 tablespoon finely chopped*
1 ounce blue cheese   *onion*

Mix all of the ingredients together in a bowl and beat until smooth. Roll the mixture into bite-size balls, chill and roll in finely chopped parsley just before serving. Serve chilled. Makes about twenty balls.

Frozen Cheese Alexander

½ cup butter   *½ teaspoon paprika*
4 ounces blue cheese   *1 teaspoon chopped chives*
1 teaspoon salt   *2 tablespoons sherry wine*

Cream the butter, add the cheese, and work until the mixture is smoothly blended. Add the remaining ingredients and stir until blended. Pack into a small gelatin mold and place into the freezer until thoroughly chilled, about one hour. Remove from the mold and serve very cold with hot toasted rye bread. Makes about one cup.

The Blue Cottage Dip

¼ cup water
1 cup small curd cottage
* cheese, creamed*
6 ounces cream cheese

½ ounce blue cheese
1 clove garlic
4 drops hot pepper sauce

Place water and cottage cheese into a blender and blend for about twenty seconds at high speed. Add the remaining ingredients and blend until smooth. Makes about two cups.

Cheese Balls

1½ cups (6 ounces)
* shredded, mild Monterey,*
* Colby, or Swiss cheese*
1 tablespoon flour

¼ teaspoon salt
Dash cayenne
3 egg whites
½ cup finely crushed crackers

Mix cheese with flour and seasoning. Beat the egg whites until stiff and add to the cheese mixture. Roll mixture into small balls and roll in the cracker crumbs until evenly coated. Deep fry until brown but not melted; drain on paper towels. Serve hot. Makes about twenty-four balls.

Monterey Spread

½ pound Monterey cheese
2 tablespoons butter
½ teaspoon salt

¼ teaspoon pepper
1 can tomato soup
2 eggs

Dice the cheese and melt in a double boiler. Blend in the butter, salt, pepper, and tomato soup and stir until smooth and heated through. Beat the eggs well and stir into the cheese mixture. Simmer until thick, stirring constantly. Serve hot on crackers or toast squares. Makes about 2¼ cups.

Anchovy Cheese Spread

8 ounces cream cheese
¼ cup butter
1 teaspoon capers
1 teaspoon paprika

2 anchovies, finely chopped
1 shallot, finely chopped
½ teaspoon caraway seeds
½ teaspoon salt

Blend cheese and butter until smooth. Add remaining ingredients and blend together. Press into a small mold and refrigerate for several hours before serving. Remove from the mold and serve with crackers. Makes about one cup.

Anchovy Cheese Dip

8 ounces cream cheese
2 tablespoons chopped
   chives
1 tablespoon ground
   anchovies or anchovy
   paste

1 tablespoon milk
1 teaspoon lemon juice
¼ teaspoon Worcestershire
   sauce

Combine all of the ingredients in a small mixing bowl and beat until smooth and fluffy. Chill and serve cold. Makes about two cups.

Lobster Dip

8 ounces cream cheese
¼ cup mayonnaise
1 clove garlic, crushed
1 teaspoon grated onion
1 teaspoon prepared mustard

1 teaspoon sugar
¼ teaspoon salt
5 ounces flaked lobster
3 tablespoons sweet, white
   wine

Melt cream cheese in a double boiler. Blend in mayonnaise, garlic, onion, mustard, sugar, and salt. Add lobster and wine, and stir until heated through. Serve hot, with toast squares or crackers. Makes 1¾ cups.

Clam Dip

8 ounces cream cheese   7 ounces minced clams
2 ounces blue cheese   (canned)
1 tablespoon chopped chives   Milk
¼ teaspoon salt

Combine cheeses, chives, and salt in a mixing bowl and beat until smooth. Stir drained clams into cheese mixture. Thin the mixture with milk to a spreadable consistency and chill. Serve chilled with crackers. Makes 1⅔ cups.

Toasted Cheese Roll-ups

6 slices freshly baked bread   ½ teaspoon seasoned salt
½ cup butter   ¼ teaspoon paprika
½ cup shredded mild
   Cheddar cheese

Cut fresh, warm bread into as thin slices as possible. Use an electric knife or a very sharp bread knife. Trim away the crusts. Cream the butter and add the cheese. Blend the butter and cheese until smooth; blend in the salt and paprika. Spread evenly on the bread slices. Roll each slice of bread into a log and fasten with toothpicks. Brown the logs under the broiler until they are evenly toasted and slightly melted. Serve hot. Makes 6 servings.

Cheese Cakes

2 tablespoons butter   ¼ teaspoon salt
3½ tablespoons flour   Small pinch of cayenne
4 tablespoons shredded mild   3 egg whites
   Cheddar cheese

Preheat the oven to 350 degrees. Melt the butter, add flour, and stir until well blended. Remove from the heat and add the cheese, salt, and cayenne. Beat the egg whites until stiff, then fold into the cheese and butter mixture. Drop by tea-spoonfuls onto a greased cookie sheet about one inch apart. Bake at 350 degrees for twelve minutes or until lightly browned. Makes 24 cakes.

Cheddar Bumps

12 two-inch squares of thickly sliced Italian bread	*1 tablespoon milk*
¼ cup bread crumbs	*1 tablespoon melted butter*
2 ounces sharp Cheddar cheese, grated	*1 egg yolk*
	Salt, pepper, and cayenne to taste

Fry the bread squares in hot oil until golden brown. Mix the bread crumbs, cheese, milk, butter, and egg yolk in a small bowl and stir until well blended. Season with salt, pepper, and cayenne to taste. Use the back of a teaspoon to press a small crater into each of the fried bread squares. Spoon the cheese mixture onto the bread squares in generous mounds. Heat gently under a broiler until very hot and well browned. Serve hot. Makes 12 servings.

Chutney Spread

½ cup butter	*⅓ cup chutney*
8 ounces sharp Cheddar cheese, grated	

Melt the butter, stir in the cheese and chutney, and stir until smooth. Cool and spread on toast squares or crackers. Makes about 1¼ cups spread.

Wine and Cheese Spread

8 ounces mild Cheddar cheese	*1 tablespoon prepared mustard*
3 tablespoons cooking sherry	*½ teaspoon salt*
2 tablespoons cream	*Cayenne*
2 tablespoons butter	

Force the cheese through a meat grinder. Add the wine, cream, butter, and seasoning and mix until creamy. Spread the mixture on crackers by forcing through a pastry tube. Makes about 1½ cups of spread.

Wellington Cheese Croquettes

3 tablespoons butter
⅓ cup flour
1 cup milk
2 egg yolks
2 tablespoons cream
2 cups diced mild Cheddar
  cheese

½ teaspoon salt
⅛ teaspoon pepper
1 cup fine bread crumbs
1 egg, lightly beaten

Melt the butter and add the flour stirring until well blended. Gradually add the milk stirring constantly. Bring the mixture to a boil and then add the lightly beaten egg yolks and cream. Blend in the cheese and season with the salt and pepper. Spread the mixture on a plate to cool. When cool, shape tablespoon-size portions into patties. Dip each patty into bread crumbs, egg, and then bread crumbs. Deep fry until brown and serve hot. Makes six servings.

Cheese Puffs

4 tablespoons flour
1 cup water
4 tablespoons grated cheese,
  Cheddar or Romano

½ teaspoon salt
⅛ teaspoon pepper
2 tablespoons butter
2 eggs

Preheat the oven to 300 degrees. Moisten the flour with a small amount of water and stir into a smooth paste. Stir the cheese, salt, and pepper into the flour mixture. Place the butter and the remaining water into a sauce pan and heat to boiling, then add the cheese and flour mixture slowly, stirring constantly. Cook the mixture about three minutes and allow to cool. When cold, beat the mixture with an electric mixer at medium speed and add the eggs one at a time. Beat for ten minutes. Lightly grease a baking sheet and drop the mixture onto the sheet in large teaspoonfuls. The puffs will triple in size so be sure to allow enough room between them. Bake at 300 degrees for twenty minutes or until golden brown. Makes about twenty-four puffs.

Cheddar Bread Sticks

*1 large loaf unsliced white
    bread
8 ounces sharp Cheddar
    cheese, shredded*

*1 cup butter
1 clove garlic, crushed*

Preheat the oven to 400 degrees. Trim the crusts from the bread and cut the loaf into one-inch-thick slices. Do not cut the slices all the way through, leave about one-half inch at the bottom to fold the slices together. Cut the loaf lengthwise also, leaving about one-half inch at the bottom to hold the halves together. Place the bread on a baking sheet. Mix one cup of the cheese, the butter, and garlic together and spread the mixture between the slices of bread. Press the slices together and sprinkle the remaining cheese on top. Bake for fifteen minutes at 400 degrees. Makes about twenty-six pieces.

Cheese Stuffed Prunes

Select large, quality prunes and stew them only until tender, drain and let them cool. When cool, remove the pits carefully so as not to break the prune. For each prune, blend about three-quarters teaspoon grated Cheddar with enough mayonnaise to produce a smooth paste. Place the cheese mixture into a pastry tube and fill each prune with the cheese mixture until it is plump and well shaped. Serve on a small, round leaf of crisp lettuce.

Fried Camembert Balls

Cut small wedges of Camembert and roll the cheese into one-half-inch balls. Roll the balls in bread crumbs, egg, and again in the bread crumbs. Deep-fry at 375 degrees until crisp and brown. Drain and serve hot. Cheddar, Swiss, or brick cheese can be substituted for Camembert.

Cheese-filled Mushrooms

*1 quart fresh mushrooms
  (large)*
1 tablespoon chopped onion
1 teaspoon oil
¼ cup finely chopped salami

*¼ cup Smoky Cheese Spread
  (recipe below)*
1 tablespoon catsup
Soft bread crumbs

Preheat the oven to 425 degrees. Wash and remove the stems from enough mushrooms to obtain two cups of large crowns. Hollow out the crowns and chop the stems to obtain three tablespoons of chopped mushroom. Cook the chopped mushroom with the onion in the oil. Add the salami, cheese, and catsup and stir in thoroughly. Stuff into the crowns and coat with the bread crumbs. Bake on a baking sheet at 425 degrees for six minutes or until hot. Makes eight servings.

Smoky Cheese Spread

*½ pound sharp Cheddar
  cheese*
¼ teaspoon dry mustard

¼ cup butter
¼ teaspoon liquid smoke
⅛ cup milk

Blend the cheese, mustard, and butter with an electric mixer. Add the liquid smoke and milk and beat until smooth. Add milk until the mixture is a loose spreading consistency. Chill. Makes about ¾ cup.

Camembert Croquettes

¼ cup flour
1 ounce ground rice (rice flour)
6 tablespoons milk
½ pound Camembert (after the rind has been removed), diced

⅓ cup butter
Salt, cayenne, and nutmeg to taste

Mix the flour, rice, and milk in the top half of double boiler and stir until smooth. Heat the mixture and add the cheese and butter. Heat slowly, stirring constantly, until the mixture is smooth and well blended. Add the salt and just a touch of nutmeg and cayenne. Spread the mixture on a plate to cool. When cool, form tablespoon-size portions into round patties. Coat the patties with bread crumbs, then egg and then bread crumbs so that they are evenly coated. Fry in deep oil at 350 degrees until very lightly browned. Serve on Melba rounds. Makes about twelve croquettes.

Chicken and Cheese Swirls

Filling:

2 cups finely diced, cooked chicken
1 cup ground rice (rice flour)

1 tablespoon chopped chives
½ teaspoon salt
⅛ teaspoon cayenne
⅛ teaspoon curry powder

Combine all of the above ingredients in a bowl and save until later.

Pastry:

1 package pie crust mix
1 cup ground rice (rice flour)
1 tablespoon chopped parsley

1 tablespoon chopped chives
5 tablespoons water
8 ounces mild Cheddar, sliced one-eighth-inch thick

Mix pie crust, rice, parsley, and chives in a bowl and blend with a fork. Add the water one tablespoon at a time until the dry ingredients are moistened and can be formed into a ball. Divide the ball in half.

Roll out one of the halves on a pastry cloth to a twelve- by sixteen-inch rectangle. Spread one half of the chicken mixture on the pastry and place four slices of cheese over the chicken in a single layer. Roll up the pastry from the end.

Make a second roll with the remaining ingredients and then chill both rolls in the refrigerator for fifteen minutes. Preheat the oven to 350 degrees. Lightly grease a baking sheet. Cut each roll into one-half-inch slices and place them on the baking sheet. Bake at 350 for fifteen minutes or until golden brown. Cool on a cake cooling rack. Makes about twenty-four pieces.

Cheese Cups

1 ½ cups milk	*Pepper to taste*
4 tablespoons semolina	*4 tablespoons grated*
8 ounces Cheddar cheese,	*Parmesan cheese*
grated	*Butter*

Boil the milk and when boiling add the semolina. Stir the mixture until smooth and thick. Add the cheese and a dash of pepper, and simmer over a low heat for five minutes, stirring constantly. Divide the mixture evenly in twelve custard cups. Sprinkle each cup with grated Parmesan and a small dab of butter. Broil gently until well browned. Makes about twelve servings.

Cheese Ramequins

1 ounce butter	*Pepper to taste*
1 tablespoon flour	*½ teaspoon powdered sugar*
1 ¼ cups milk	*8 egg yolks*
⅔ cup light cream	*8 egg whites*
8 ounces grated Parmesan	*¾ teaspoon salt*

Preheat the oven to 325 degrees. Melt the butter in a saucepan, and when melted stir in the flour and salt until blended. Mix the milk and cream together in another saucepan and bring to a boil. Slowly add the milk to the butter and flour mixture, stirring constantly until smooth. Remove from the heat and add the cheese, a dash of pepper, one-half teaspoon of powdered sugar and the egg yolks. Mix well. In a separate bowl beat the egg whites until stiff. Add one-quarter of the beaten egg whites to the cheese mixture and when well mixed add the remaining egg whites. Stir to the consistency of cream. Place twelve paper baking cups into a muffin tin and fill each about three-quarters full. Bake at 325 degrees for eighteen minutes or until set. Makes twelve servings.

Beef and Cheese Bites

Pastry for two nine-inch pie crusts	*⅔ cup minced onion greens*
1 pound ground beef	*6 eggs*
1 teaspoon salt	*2½ cups light cream*
3 cups shredded Swiss cheese, about 12 ounces	*¾ teaspoon salt*
	¼ teaspoon sugar
	⅛ teaspoon cayenne

Preheat the oven to 425 degrees. Roll the pastry into a seventeen-by twelve-inch rectangle. Line a jelly roll pan (15× 10×1 inch) with the pastry and trim off the edges. Brown the ground beef in a large skillet. Add the salt, mix in and drain on paper towels. Place the cheese, onion, and ground beef into the pastry-lined pan in layers. Mix the eggs, cream, salt, sugar, and pepper in a bowl and beat thoroughly. Slowly pour the mixture over the ground beef. Bake for fifteen minutes at 425 degrees. Reduce the oven temperatures to 300 and bake for fifteen more minutes or until a knife inserted into the middle comes out clean. Allow to cool for at least ten minutes, then cut into one and one-quarter-inch squares. Serve warm. Makes ninety-six pieces.

SANDWICHES

The Tuna Cottage

1 cup small curd cottage   ¼ cup chopped celery
*   cheese, creamed and salted   ¼ cup chopped onion greens*
1 seven-ounce can tuna,   5 radishes, diced
*   drained and flaked   Salt and pepper to taste*
½ cup mayonnaise   6 English muffins

Combine the first eight ingredients in a small bowl and mix well. Split the muffins and toast them. Spread the mixture on six muffin halves and cover with the remaining halves. Makes six servings.

The TV Special Sandwich

1 slice bread, buttered   ¼ inch-slice sweet onion
⅛ inch-thick slice of Colby   ⅓ cup ground beef
*   cheese   Salt to taste*

Place the layers on the bread as listed and sprinkle with salt. Broil until the ground meat is done and the cheese slightly melted. Makes one sandwich.

The Pizzaburger

1 pound ground beef   ⅛ teaspoon pepper
¼ cup chopped onion   6 ounces mozzarella cheese,
1 teaspoon salt   6 slices
½ teaspoon garlic salt   6 hamburger rolls, sliced and
½ teaspoon basil   buttered
¼ teaspoon crushed orégano

Mix the beef, onion, salt, garlic salt, basil, orégano, and pepper in a small bowl. Divide the mixture into six equal portions and shape into patties. Broil the patties until the beef is done to your taste. Place a slice of mozzarella cheese on each patty and return to the broiler just long enough to melt the cheese. Serve on the rolls. Serves six.

The Vertical Hero

Cut four slices of fresh Italian bread. Sprinkle each slice with malt vinegar, olive oil, and orégano. Place two slices of bologna, canned pimiento, and chopped green pepper on the first slice of bread. Top with the second slice of bread.

On the second layer place shredded lettuce, sliced tomatoes, chopped, hard-cooked eggs, and anchovies. Top with the third slice of bread.

Place cooked salami, caciocavallo cheese, and onion slice on the third layer. Top with the remaining slice of bread and skewer the sandwich to hold it together. Makes one sandwich for a big eater.

The Hot Brick

¼ cup butter
2 tablespoons prepared
* mustard*
2 teaspoons poppy seeds
2 tablespoons chopped
* onions*

4 hamburger rolls
4 slices boiled ham
4 slices brick cheese, about
* four ounces*

Preheat the oven to 350 degrees. Mix the butter, mustard, poppy seeds, and onions in a small bowl. Slice the hamburger rolls and spread the mixture over the cut surfaces. Place a layer of ham and a layer of cheese on the bottom half of each bun and cover with the top half. Place the buns on a baking sheet and bake at 350 degrees for about twenty minutes or until heated through. Makes four servings.

Caesar's Grilled Cheese

10 ounces mozzarella cheese, shredded	2 tablespoons chopped chives
3 ounces hard salami, diced into small cubes	⅔ cup milk
¼ cup chopped green pepper	3 eggs
	12 thin slices Italian bread

Place the cheese into a small bowl. Chop the salami into fine chunks and add to the cheese. Add the green pepper and chives and mix the ingredients thoroughly. Place the milk and eggs into a shallow bowl and beat them slightly. Dip a slice of bread into the egg mixture and then transfer it to a hot, buttered grill. Spoon about one-half cup of the cheese onto the bread while it is browning. Dip a second slice of bread into the egg and place this slice, dipped side up, on top of the cheese mixture. Turn the sandwich over when brown and brown on the other side until the cheese is melted. Repeat with the remaining bread to make six servings.

Toasted Mushroom Sandwich

3 tablespoons butter	Salt and pepper
¼ cup flour	Paprika
1 cup light cream	8 slices day-old Italian bread, thinly sliced
8 ounces Cheddar cheese, shredded	
6 ounces mushrooms, cleaned and chopped	

Melt the butter and stir in the flour until well blended. Slowly add one cup of light cream, stirring constantly. Sauté the mushrooms. Bring the cream and butter mixture to a boil and then add the mushrooms. Blend in the cheese until the mixture is smooth and spreadable. Season to taste with salt, pepper, and paprika.

Cut 8 thin slices from a day-old Italian bread and remove the crusts. Spread the mushroom mixture over four slices and cover with the remaining slices. Grill the sandwich in butter on both sides until brown and very hot. Makes four servings.

Nut and Cheese Sandwich

¼ cup grated brick cheese   *2 slices bread*
¼ cup chopped walnuts

Mix the cheese and nuts together until well blended. A small amount of mayonnaise may be added to moisten the mixture if needed. Spread between bread slices. Makes one sandwich.

The Egg Sandwich

1 hard-cooked egg   *2 teaspoons mayonnaise*
¼ cup shredded Monterey   *Salt and pepper*
cheese

Chop the egg very finely, then add the cheese and mayonnaise. Blend all ingredients thoroughly and season with salt and pepper to taste. Spread on whole wheat bread. Makes one sandwich.

Cheese and Anchovy Sandwich

2 tablespoons butter   *Paprika*
¼ cup grated, mild Cheddar   *Mustard*
cheese   *Anchovy sauce to taste*
1 teaspoon vinegar   *Pumpernickel bread*
Salt

Combine the first three ingredients in a small bowl. Blend in the seasonings. Spread between thin slices of Pumpernickel bread. Makes one serving.

Italian Sausage Hero

1½ loaves French bread	*2 cups chopped green pepper*
12 Italian sausages	*2 cups chopped, sweet red*
½ cup water	*pepper*
2 tablespoons cooking oil	*Catsup to taste*
1½ cups sliced onions	*6 slices caciocavallo cheese*
1¼ cups sliced mushrooms	

Split the French bread lengthwise without cutting through. Prick each sausage several times and place them into a skillet. Add the water and bring to a boil. Cover the pan and simmer slowly for about fifteen minutes. Uncover the pan, drain the excess liquid, and brown the sausages, turning often. Push the sausages to one side of the pan and add the oil, onions, mushrooms, and peppers. Stir to coat with oil. Sauté until the onions are clear. Place the sausages into the split bread. Spread the onion mixture evenly over the sausages. Add catsup to taste. Cover the onions with slices of caciocavallo and place under a broiler until the cheese is just melted. Cut between each sausage to make twelve servings.

French Fried Ham and Cheese

4 ounces Swiss cheese, finely	*½ teaspoon salt*
grated	*1 tablespoon butter*
¼ cup light cream	*1 tablespoon flour*
8 pieces thinly sliced Vienna	*½ teaspoon garlic powder*
bread	*1 cup milk*
8 slices boiled ham	*4 ounces shredded medium-*
2 eggs	*sharp Cheddar cheese*
¼ cup milk	

Stir together Swiss cheese and cream until smooth. Spread equally on each slice of bread. Place two slices of ham on four slices of bread and cover with remaining four slices of bread to form a sandwich. In a shallow bowl beat the two eggs slightly and stir in the milk and salt. Dip each side of the sandwich into the egg-milk mixture and fry on a well-buttered griddle until brown and melted. Serve with the following cheese sauce: Melt the 1 tablespoon butter and stir in the flour and garlic powder. Remove from the heat and stir in the milk. Heat the mixture to boiling, stirring constantly. Boil for one minute, slowly stir in the cheese until melted. Pour the hot sauce over the sandwiches. Makes four servings.

Hamburgers with Blue Cheese

1½ pounds ground beef
½ cup red wine
1 teaspoon salt
2 teaspoons butter
2 teaspoons salad oil
4 hamburger buns
3 ounces blue cheese
½ cup cultured cream

Combine ground beef, red wine, and salt. Mix gently with a fork until blended. Make into four patties of equal size and about one inch thick. Heat the butter and oil on a griddle over medium heat until the butter is foamy. Place the patties in the butter and fry for one minute. Cook until done, turning frequently. Patties will take about eight minutes to get medium-well done. Split and toast the buns. In a small saucepan combine the crumbled blue cheese and the cultured cream. Heat until lukewarm. Place the patties on the bottom half of each bun and top with the cheese mixture. Cover with the tops of buns and serve. Makes four servings.

The Tuna Hero

2 seven-ounce cans of tuna,
* drained and flaked*
¼ cup cultured cream
¼ cup chopped parsley
½ cup mayonnaise
1 tablespoon lemon juice
½ teaspoon garlic salt
1 long loaf of French bread
3 tablespoons butter
4 ounces Swiss cheese

Preheat the oven to 350 degrees. Combine tuna, cultured cream, parsley, mayonnaise, lemon juice, and garlic in a small bowl. Slice the bread in half lengthwise and butter both halves. Slice the Swiss cheese into thin slices and spread in a layer on the bread. Spoon on the tuna mixture evenly and cover with the top half of the bread. Bake at 350 degrees for twenty-five minutes. Serves six.

Mozzarella in Carozza

2 one-eighth-inch-thick slices of white bread	*2 eggs*
	¼ teaspoon salt
1 one-quarter-inch-thick slice of mozzarella cheese about two inches square	*Oil*

Trim the crusts from the bread to about a three-inch square. Place the cheese on the bread and cover with the second slice to form a sandwich. Beat the eggs and salt in a shallow bowl. Soak the sandwich in the egg for fifteen minutes on each side. Remove the sandwich from the egg and pinch the edges together to seal the cheese in. Fry the sandwich in hot oil until brown. Serve hot. Makes one sandwich.

Broiled Cheese and Bacon

2 medium onions, thinly sliced	*12 ounces mild Cheddar cheese*
2 tablespoons butter	*3 strips of crisply fried bacon*
¼ teaspoon salt	*6 green pepper rings*
6 thin slices sandwich bread	
6 tablespoons prepared chili sauce	

Sauté the onions in butter and salt. Toast and butter the bread. Spread one tablespoon of chili sauce on each slice of bread. Divide the onions evenly between the six sandwiches. Cut the cheese into six thick slices and place one slice on each sandwich. Crumble one-half strip of bacon over each slice of cheese and add a ring of green pepper. Broil until the cheese is melted and serve hot. Makes six servings.

The Super Denver Sandwich

½ loaf French bread
⅔ cup deviled ham
4 eggs
¼ cup milk
¼ teaspoon salt
Pepper to taste

¼ cup chopped chives
2 tablespoons butter
1 medium tomato
4 ounces sharp Cheddar
    cheese

Slice the bread in half lengthwise and toast it. Spread the cut side evenly with the deviled ham. Combine the eggs, milk, salt, and a dash of pepper in a bowl and heat thoroughly. Add the chives and stir the mixture. Melt the butter in a skillet; when melted, pour in the egg mixture. Cook the eggs gently, like scrambled eggs, until they are set but still moist. Spread the eggs over the deviled ham and place four slices of tomato on top. Cover each tomato slice with a thick slice of cheese and broil slowly until the cheese is melted. Makes four servings.

Blue Cheese and Fruit Sandwich

24 slices of date and nut
    bread, about two inches
    square
8 ounces cream cheese
2 ounces blue cheese

½ cup walnuts, chopped
1 twenty-nine-ounce can of
    pear halves
24 maraschino cherry halves
Paprika

Butter each slice of bread. In a small bowl mix the cream cheese and blue cheese together and stir in the walnuts. Spread the mixture over the bread and add a pear slice to each sandwich. Garnish with a cherry half and a dash of paprika. Makes twenty-four servings.

The Hero Sandwich

1 loaf Vienna bread
¼ cup cultured cream
2 tablespoons mustard
⅛ teaspoon garlic powder
Lettuce leaves
8 slices caciocavallo cheese
  (about 8 ounces)

8 slices bologna
8 ounces Colby cheese, sliced
Tomato slices
12 slices cooked salami
8 ounces Swiss cheese, sliced
Sweet onion rings

Cut the bread in half lengthwise. Combine the cultured cream, mustard, and garlic powder; spread on the bread. Place lettuce leaves over the bottom half of the bread. Place the caciocavallo cheese, bologna, Colby cheese, tomato slices, salami, Swiss cheese, and onion rings on top of the lettuce in layers. Cover with the other half of the bread and cut into four to six sandwiches. Makes four to six servings.

Chicken and Cheese Double-decker Open-faced Sandwich

1½ cups chopped cooked
  chicken
1 hard-cooked egg, chopped
¾ cup chopped celery
¼ cup pickle relish
¼ cup mayonnaise
Salt to taste
1 egg

8 ounces aged brick cheese,
  shredded
2 tablespoons mayonnaise
1 tablespoon prepared
  mustard
Butter
12 slices sandwich bread

Combine the chicken, chopped egg, chopped celery, relish, and mayonnaise in a small bowl, add salt and set aside. In a second bowl beat the egg and mix in the cheese. Blend thoroughly with an electric mixer and add the mayonnaise and mustard. Blend until smooth. Spread the chicken mixture on six slices of buttered bread. Butter the remaining six slices and place on top of the chicken to form a sandwich. Place under the broiler until brown on one side. Remove and turn the sandwich over. Spread the cheese mixture on the untoasted side, dividing it evenly. Return to the oven and broil gently until the cheese mixture is slightly brown and melted. Makes six servings.

SOUPS

White Cheese Soup

1 tablespoon finely chopped
*   onions*
1 tablespoon butter
1¼ cups hot water
2½ cups milk

2 tablespoons flour
Salt and pepper to taste
2 tablespoons finely grated
*   Cheddar or Parmesan*
*   cheese*

Sauté the onions in butter only until clear, do not brown the onions. When the onions are soft add the hot water. When the onions are fully cooked, add the milk and bring to a boil. Mix a small amount of milk with the flour and stir to form a smooth paste. When the milk boils add the flour mixture and stir until smooth. Add salt and pepper to taste and simmer until it thickens. Just before serving, stir the grated cheese into the soup. Serve very hot. Makes six servings.

Zuppa Pavese

5 cups chicken or vegetable
*   consommé*
8 very thin slices of French
*   bread*
Butter

4 eggs
8 teaspoons of grated
*   Parmesan or sharp*
*   Cheddar cheese*

Heat the consommé. Fry the slices of bread in butter until brown. When the consommé is hot, poach the eggs in it. Drain the eggs and place one egg into each bowl. Pour the consommé over the eggs and add two slices of bread to each bowl. Sprinkle two teaspoons of cheese over the bread in each bowl. Serve very hot. Makes four servings.

Asparagus Soup

2 tablespoons butter
2 tablespoons flour
1 teaspoon salt
Dash of nutmeg
Pepper
3 cups milk
10 ounces of fresh asparagus
    tips cut into one-half inch
    lengths, cooked and
    drained

6 ounces mild Cheddar
    cheese, shredded
Paprika
3 teaspoons grated Parmesan
    cheese

Melt the butter and stir in the flour, salt, nutmeg, and pepper. Add all of the milk. Cook, stirring constantly, until the mixture is thick and bubbly. Add the cooked asparagus and Cheddar cheese; stir until the cheese has melted. Divide into six servings and garnish each bowl with paprika and one half teaspoon of grated Parmesan cheese. Serve hot. Makes four servings.

Chicken with Cheese Soup

4 slices bacon
¼ cup chopped onions
2 tablespoons chopped green
    pepper
2 cups milk
1 can condensed cream of
    chicken soup

1 cup diced cooked chicken
Salt to taste
4 ounces Colby cheese,
    shredded
Mace

Cook the bacon until crisp, drain, and crumble two of the slices. Pour two tablespoons of bacon grease into a saucepan and add the onions and green pepper. Cook the onions and pepper until they are tender. Add the milk, soup, chicken, a dash of salt, and the crumbled bacon. Cook until thoroughly heated. Add the shredded cheese and stir until the cheese is melted. Pour into four bowls and garnish each bowl with one half slice of the remaining bacon and a dash of mace. Makes four servings.

Cheese and Onion Soup

3 tablespoons butter	*8 ounces medium-sharp*
1 cup chopped, sweet onions	*Cheddar cheese, shredded*
3 tablespoons flour	*6 rounds of toast, buttered*
½ teaspoon salt	*6 teaspoons grated Parmesan*
Pepper to taste	*cheese*
4 cups milk	

Melt the butter and add the onions. Cook only until clear and do not brown. When the onions are tender stir in the flour, salt, and a dash of pepper. Cook until the mixture thickens, stirring constantly. Add the milk and cheese, stirring until the cheese melts. Divide the mixture into six bowls and float a round of toast in each bowl. Spoon a teaspoon of Parmesan cheese on each round and place the bowls under the broiler until the cheese is well browned. Serve immediately. Makes six servings.

Chicken and Cheese Chowder

1 cup shredded carrot	*1 tablespoon dry white wine*
¼ cup chopped onions	*½ teaspoon celery seed*
4 tablespoons butter	*½ teaspoon Worcestershire*
¼ cup flour	*sauce*
2 cups milk	*4 ounces medium-sharp*
1¾ cups chicken broth	*Cheddar cheese, shredded*
1 cup diced cooked chicken	

In a large saucepan, cook the carrot and onions in the butter until they are tender. Do not brown the onions. When the vegetables are tender stir in the flour until the mixture is smooth. Slowly add the milk and chicken broth. Cook gently, stirring constantly, until the mixture thickens. Stir in the chicken, wine, celery seed, and Worcestershire sauce and heat until thoroughly hot. Add the cheese and stir constantly until the cheese has melted. Serve very hot. Makes four servings.

Onion Soup au Gratin

4 large onions, thinly sliced
4 tablespoons butter
4 cans (10½ ounce)
   condensed beef broth
½ cup dry sherry
2 teaspoons Worcestershire
   sauce

Dash of pepper
6 slices French bread, about
   one-half inch thick
¾ cup grated Parmesan
   cheese
6 slices Swiss cheese, about
   one-half ounce each

Cook the onions in butter, in a large saucepan, until they are tender but not brown. When the onions are done, add the beef broth, sherry, Worcestershire sauce, and pepper and bring the mixture to a boil. Pour the mixture into six oven-proof bowls. Toast the French bread and float one slice in each bowl. Sprinkle each slice of bread with about six teaspoons of Parmesan cheese and place a slice of Swiss cheese on the top. Place the bowl under the broiler and heat until the cheese is well melted and browned. Makes six servings.

ENTRÉES

I will begin this section with the recipes for several variations of rabbit; Welsh, oyster, cream, and a few more. For those of you who have been calling Welsh rabbit, Welsh *rabbit* for years and have taken much abuse because of your pronunciation, take heart, you have been right. According to Webster a Welsh rabbit is "A dish, variously made, of melted or toasted cheese, often mixed with ale or beer, poured over toasted bread or crackers;—a jocose term, like 'Cape Cod Turkey' (codfish), that through failure to recognize the joke is commonly modified in cookbooks to Welsh rarebit." And so, with our heads held high, let us proceed with four variations of Welsh rabbit.

Welsh Rabbit I

½ cup beer or ale
2 teaspoons Worcestershire
  sauce
½ teaspoon dry mustard

Dash cayenne and paprika
1 pound sharp Cheddar
  cheese, shredded
Hot toast

Place the beer into a saucepan and heat with a very low heat until it is hot. Add the seasonings and stir until well mixed. Add the cheese slowly and stir until the cheese has melted. Pour over hot toast. Makes six servings.

Welsh Rabbit II

1 tablespoon butter
8 ounces mild Cheddar or
  Monterey cheese, shredded
¼ teaspoon salt
½ teaspoon mustard

Dash of cayenne
½ cup beer or ale
1 egg
Hot toast

Melt butter in a chafing dish and when melted, add the cheese and seasonings. Stir constantly as the cheese melts. Begin adding the beer as soon as the cheese begins to melt. Add the beer very slowly, stirring constantly. Beat the egg slightly and add to the cheese mixture after all of the cheese has melted. Pour over hot toast. Makes six servings.

Welsh Rabbit III sans Beer

½ *pound Cheddar cheese,*   ½ *teaspoon prepared*
  shredded   *mustard*
¼ *cup cream*   *Hot toast*
1 *teaspoon Worcestershire*
  sauce

Melt the cheese in the top of a double boiler. When the cheese has melted, gradually add the cream, stirring constantly. Add the seasonings and when very hot serve over hot toast. Makes about four servings.

Welsh Rabbit IV sans Beer

1 *tablespoon butter*   ¼ *teaspoon salt*
1 *teaspoon cornstarch*   ¼ *teaspoon dry mustard*
½ *cup light cream*   *Dash of cayenne*
8 *ounces mild Cheddar or*   *Hot toast*
  Monterey cheese, shredded

Melt the butter in a saucepan and when melted, add the cornstarch, stirring constantly until smooth. Add the cream gradually and stir for two minutes. Add the cheese slowly, stirring constantly, until the cheese has melted. Add the seasonings and when hot pour over toast. Makes four to six servings.

The trick in preparing any rabbit is to make the cheese come out smooth and creamy, never stringy. If the cheese has a tendency to become stringy you can add a slightly beaten egg to the rabbit to relieve the problem. Using a richer grade of cheese will also eliminate the stringy cheese problem.

Tomato Rabbit

2 tablespoons butter	8 ounces mild Cheddar
2 tablespoons flour	cheese, shredded
¾ cup light cream	2 eggs, slightly beaten
¾ cup stewed tomatoes,	Salt
strained	Dry mustard to taste
⅛ teaspoon baking soda	Hot toast

Melt the butter in a chafing dish and when melted stir in the flour until smooth. Gradually pour on the cream and as soon as the mixture thickens add the tomatoes with the baking soda mixed into them. Add the cheese and eggs and stir until the cheese has melted. Stir in the seasonings and serve over toast at once. Makes about six servings.

Oyster Rabbit

1 cup fresh oysters	8 ounces mild Monterey
2 tablespoons butter	cheese, shredded
¼ teaspoon salt	2 eggs
Dash of cayenne	Hot toast

Clean and parboil the oysters. Drain and save the liquid. Remove the tough muscle from the oysters and discard it. Melt the butter and add the seasonings, stirring until well blended. Add the cheese and stir constantly until the cheese has melted. Add the liquid from cooking the oysters and the eggs, slightly beaten. Stir the mixture until smooth and then add the soft parts of the oysters. Serve on toast. Makes about six servings.

Welsh Rabbit Camembert

Here is an excellent recipe to make use of a Camembert cheese that is not destined to become a great cheese.

1 thick slice of white bread
Bacon fat
4 ounces of unripened
  Camembert cheese, cut up
1 tablespoon butter

Pepper to taste
Celery salt
1 teaspoon sautéed green
  pepper

Fry the bread in the bacon fat until it is very crisp. Place the cheese into a saucepan and heat it gently. Add the butter, a dash of pepper, and a dash of celery salt. Stir constantly until completely melted and smooth. Spread the mixture over the fried bread and broil quickly to brown the cheese. Garnish with sautéed green pepper and serve hot. Makes one serving.

Cream Rabbit

1 tablespoon butter
1 cup milk
1 teaspoon salt
¼ teaspoon pepper

6 eggs
3 ounces cream cheese
Toast rounds or crackers

Place the butter into a chafing dish and when melted add the milk and seasonings. Beat the eggs slightly and add to the milk mixture. Cook to the consistency of moist scrambled eggs. When nearly done, add the cream cheese and stir until the mixture is smooth. Serve on toast rounds or crackers. Makes about four servings.

Spanish Rabbit

2 tablespoons chopped green pepper	*2½ cups canned, whole kernel corn, drained*
2 tablespoons butter	*1 egg, well beaten*
8 ounces of canned tomatoes	*½ cup soft bread crumbs*
8 ounces Cheddar cheese, shredded	*¼ teaspoon chili powder*
	Hot toast

Cook the green pepper in the butter until it is tender. Add the tomatoes and cheese and stir until the cheese had melted. Add the corn and egg to the tomato mixture. Add the remaining ingredients and stir constantly until the mixture is heated through. Serve hot over toast. Makes six servings.

This should provide you with enough rabbits to overrun a small continent.

Veal Parmigiano

3 tablespoons butter	*1 egg, slightly beaten*
½ cup bread crumbs	*1 cup tomato sauce*
¼ cup grated Parmesan cheese	*½ teaspoon orégano*
½ teaspoon salt	*Dash of onion salt*
Dash of pepper	*4 ounces mozzarella cheese, thinly sliced*
1 pound veal cutlet, cut no more than one-quarter inch thick	

Preheat the oven to 400 degrees. Melt the butter in a ten by six by one and one-half inch baking dish. Mix the bread crumbs, Parmesan cheese, salt, and pepper together in a shallow pan. Dip the cutlets into the egg and then into the bread crumbs until thoroughly coated. Lay the cutlets into the baking dish. Bake for twenty minutes at 400 degrees, turn the meat, and bake for another fifteen minutes or until the meat is tender. Combine the tomato sauce, orégano, and onion salt in a saucepan and heat to boiling, stirring constantly. Pour the sauce over the meat and top with the mozzarella cheese. Return to the oven just long enough to melt the cheese. Makes four servings.

Veal Cutlets I

4 cutlets of veal, the cutlets should be no more than one-quarter inch thick and should weigh about 4 ounces each	*Salt and pepper to taste*
	3 tablespoons butter
	3 ounces dry red wine
	2 ounces Parmesan cheese, grated
¼ cup flour	*6 tablespoons beef stock*

Dip the cutlets in a mixture of the flour and seasonings. Place the butter in a skillet and brown the cutlets quickly. Remove the skillet from the heat, remove the cutlets, and add the wine to the skillet. Moisten the cheese with two tablespoons of the beef stock and spread the mixture over the cutlets. Add the remaining stock to the skillet and stir together until the mixture is smooth. Return the cutlets to the skillet with the cheese up, cover the pan, and simmer gently for about five minutes. Remove the cutlets to a platter and pour the sauce over them. Makes four servings.

Veal Cutlets II

1 egg	*½ cup flour*
1 tablespoon milk	*1 cup bread crumbs*
1 tablespoon oil	*4 ounces Swiss cheese, grated*
Salt and pepper to taste	*4 slices boiled ham*
4 veal cutlets, cut one-quarter inch thick	*4 tablespoons butter*

Beat the egg slightly with the milk and oil. Season each cutlet on one side with salt and pepper. Dip the seasoned side of the cutlet into the flour, the egg mixture, and then into the bread crumbs. Place one quarter of the grated cheese on the uncoated side of each cutlet and top with a slice of ham. Cook in butter, with the bread crumb side down, over a low heat for about fifteen minutes. Makes four servings.

Veal Cutlets Italian Style

4 ounces mozzarella cheese,
  4 slices
4 veal cutlets
6 ounces red wine
4 tablespoons butter

Salt and pepper to taste
Flour
Chopped parsley
Orégano

Preheat the oven to 350 degrees. Lay a slice of cheese on each cutlet and roll the meat carefully; skewer to hold together. Lay the rolls into a baking dish and add the wine and butter. Add salt and pepper and bake at 350 degrees for thirty minutes or until the meat is tender. Remove the meat from the baking dish and thicken the sauce with flour until it is smooth and creamy. Add chopped parsley and orégano to taste, and pour the sauce over the rolls of meat. Makes four servings.

Swiss Veal

6 veal cutlets
12 slices Swiss cheese, three
  by one and a half by one
  eighth inch
12 slices boiled ham, three
  by one and a half by one
  eighth inch
2 tablespoons flour

¼ teaspoon paprika
2 tablespoons vegetable
  shortening
1 can condensed cream of
  mushroom soup
1 cup light cream
¼ cup sweet white wine

Pound each cutlet into a very thin rectangle. Place two slices of cheese and two slices of ham on each cutlet alternately. Fold the veal over the ham and cheese slices and seal the edges with toothpicks. Roll the veal in a mixture of flour and paprika until well coated. Heat the shortening in a skillet and brown the cutlets in the hot grease. When nicely browned, add the remaining ingredients to the skillet, cover, and simmer for thirty minutes or until the veal is tender. Makes six servings.

Broiled Fish with Cheese

2 pounds of fish fillets
3 tablespoons melted butter
4 ounces of Cheddar cheese, shredded
2 tablespoons chili sauce

1 tablespoon prepared mustard
1½ teaspoons prepared horseradish

Place fish on a broiler pan and brush with the melted butter. Broil eight to ten minutes, until browned or until the fish can be easily flaked with a fork. Blend the remaining ingredients in a small bowl and spread the mixture over the broiled fish. Return the fish to the broiler and heat until the cheese is melted and lightly browned. Makes six servings.

Perch with Parmesan

½ cup butter
1 egg
¼ cup milk
1 cup cracker crumbs

⅓ cup grated Parmesan
⅛ teaspoon pepper
1 pound perch fillets

Preheat the oven to 425 degrees. Place the butter into a baking dish and melt. Beat the egg together with the milk in a shallow pan. In another pan mix the crumbs, cheese, and pepper. Dip each fillet in the crumb mixture, then in the egg mixture, and once again in the crumb mixture. Place the fillets into the buttered pan. Bake for ten minutes at 425 degrees, turn the fillets, and bake for another ten minutes or until golden brown. Makes four servings.

Turbot with Cheese Sauce

1 turbot, about two pounds
4 ounces dry white wine
1 cup butter
2 tablespoons lemon juice
Salt and pepper to taste
1½ pounds mushrooms
⅛ cup cooking oil

⅛ cup butter
¾ to 1 cup flour
2 eggs
2 tablespoons heavy cream
8 ounces Cheddar cheese,
  grated

Preheat the oven to 350 degrees. Place the fish into a baking dish. Pour the wine over the fish and add the butter. Add the lemon juice, and salt and pepper to taste. Cover the dish with aluminum foil and bake at 350 degrees until the fish is just beginning to come away from the bones. While the fish is baking, dice the mushrooms and cook them in the oil and butter. Season the mushrooms very lightly with salt and pepper. When the mushrooms are cooked, add the flour and turn up the heat to bring the mixture to the boiling point. Simmer the flour and mushrooms until all of the liquid has been absorbed. In a separate bowl, beat the eggs and cream until they are well blended; stir in the cheese and add salt and pepper to taste. Remove the fish from the oven and lift off the foil. Spread the mushroom mixture over the fish and the cheese sauce on top of the mushrooms. Place the dish under the broiler and heat it slowly until the cheese sauce is browned and very hot. Makes four servings.

Chicken Parmesan

2½ pounds roasting chicken,
jointed
1 tablespoon olive oil
Salt and pepper to taste
½ cup plus two tablespoons
chicken stock
1¼ cups White Sauce (recipe
below)

3 ounces grated Parmesan
cheese
2 egg yolks
2 tablespoons heavy cream
¼ cup bread crumbs

Place the chicken and oil into a skillet and brown the chicken lightly. Add the salt and pepper to taste and pour on the chicken stock. Cover the pan and cook over a low heat for about twenty minutes. While the chicken cooks, prepare the White Sauce, below.

Preheat the oven to 450 degrees. Sprinkle an ovenproof baking dish with part of the cheese and arrange the pieces of chicken in the dish. Add the white sauce to the mixture in the skillet and stir. Add all but one tablespoon of the cheese to the sauce and stir until the cheese has melted. Beat the egg yolks slightly and add to the sauce; add the cream. Stir the mixture constantly until the sauce thickens and is smooth. Pour the sauce over the chicken and sprinkle with the remaining cheese and bread crumbs. Bake for ten minutes at 450 degrees or until brown. Makes four servings.

White Sauce

2 tablespoons butter
2 tablespoons flour
¼ teaspoon salt

Dash pepper
1 cup milk, scalded

Melt the butter in a saucepan and add the flour and seasonings. Stir until the mixture is well blended and smooth.

Gradually add the scalded milk to the butter mixture, stirring constantly with a wire whisk. The whisk is the most efficient tool for blending this type of sauce and many others. Bring the mixture to a boil and let boil for two minutes, stirring constantly. Keep the sauce warm until ready to use. Makes 1¼ cups.

Roast Chicken with Cream Cheese

1 three to three and one   *Salt and pepper to taste*
  half pound chicken for   *8 ounces cream cheese*
  roasting   *5 ounces light cream*

Preheat the oven to 350 degrees. Place the chicken into a baking dish and rub inside with salt. Season the outside with salt and pepper to taste. Beat the cream cheese until light and fluffy. Stuff the chicken with the cream cheese and place the chicken in the oven to bake. Bake about twenty minutes per pound or until the meat is tender. Baste the chicken every ten minutes with the cream. Makes five to six servings.

Chicken Rolls

¼ cup chopped onions   *6 whole chicken breasts,*
½ cup chopped mushrooms   *boneless*
2 tablespoons butter   *Flour*
2 tablespoons flour   *2 eggs, slightly beaten*
½ cup light cream   *¾ cup very fine bread*
¼ teaspoon salt   *crumbs*
Dash of cayenne
5 ounces sharp Cheddar
  cheese, shredded

Cook the onions and mushrooms gently in butter in a sauté pan. When the mushrooms are done add the flour and stir until smooth. Add the cream, stirring constantly. Stir in the seasonings and cook until the mixture is very thick. Slowly add the cheese, stirring constantly, until all of the cheese has melted. Pour the mixture into a baking dish and chill in the refrigerator until the mixture is firm and can be shaped. Cut the cheese mixture into six equal portions and shape them into short logs.

Remove the skin from the chicken and place it on a board with the boned side up. Pound the meat into cutlets about one-quarter inch thick. Salt each piece and place a cheese log on each. Reshape the logs, if necessary, to make them short enough to be enclosed by the chicken. Roll the chicken around the cheese carefully; seal the edges carefully to prevent the cheese mixture from escaping when it melts. Dust the rolls of chicken lightly with flour. Dip them in the beaten eggs and roll them in bread crumbs to coat them evenly. Chill the chicken rolls for at least one hour before cooking.

Preheat the oven to 325 degrees. Remove the chicken rolls from the refrigerator and deep fry for about five minutes or until brown. Drain the chicken on paper towels. Place the rolls into a baking dish and bake at 325 degrees for thirty to forty-five minutes or until tender. Makes six servings.

Potatoes au Gratin I

2 pounds round white
    potatoes
2 ounces boiled ham,
    chopped
2 tablespoons butter
1 egg, well beaten

Salt and pepper to taste
1¼ cups White Sauce (see
    Index)
1 ounce Cheddar cheese,
    grated

Preheat the oven to 425 degrees. Boil the potatoes in their skins, peel them, and cut them in half. Scoop out the center of each half and place in a mixing bowl. To the scooped-out potato add the ham, butter, and the beaten egg. Mix with an electric mixer until the mixture is thoroughly blended. Mix in the salt and pepper. Fill each of the scooped-out potato shells with this mixture heaping it on top. Stand the shells upright in a buttered baking dish and pour the White Sauce around the potatoes. Sprinkle the potatoes with the grated cheese and bake only until the top is well browned. Makes six to eight servings.

Potatoes au Gratin II

*1 pound raw potatoes,
  peeled
1 egg
1½ cups boiling milk
1 teaspoon salt
¼ teaspoon white pepper*

*Dash nutmeg
1 ounce Swiss cheese, grated
1 slice of onion
3 tablespoons butter
2 tablespoons grated Swiss
  cheese*

Preheat the oven to 450 degrees. Slice the potatoes into thin slices. Beat the egg and mix with the potatoes. Add the boiling milk, seasonings, and cheese and blend. Rub a deep baking dish with the onion and then coat the dish with one half of the butter. Place the potato mixture into the baking dish and distribute them evenly. Sprinkle with the remaining cheese and the rest of the butter in small dabs. Bake at 450 degrees for about forty-five minutes or until the potatoes are soft. Makes four servings.

Pan-fried Potatoes and Cheese

*1 pound potatoes
½ pound onions
¼ cup bacon drippings*

*¼ pound Cheddar cheese,
  shredded
Salt and pepper to taste*

Peel the potatoes, wash, and slice into very thin slices. Peel the onions and slice these also into thin slices. Heat the bacon drippings in a skillet and when hot use one half of the potatoes and place them in an overlapping layer on the bottom of the skillet. Next place the onions over the potatoes in an even layer. Spread the shredded cheese evenly over the onions and top the cheese with the remaining potatoes. Season each layer with salt and pepper. Fry gently until almost cooked through. Remove the skillet from the heat and place under a broiler. Broil very slowly until the top layer of potatoes are soft and well browned. Remove from the pan and serve in quarter pie sections. Makes four servings.

Parmesan Soufflé

1 tablespoon butter
2 tablespoons flour
2 cups milk
4 tablespoons grated
  Parmesan cheese

4 egg yolks
6 egg whites
Salt and cayenne to taste

Preheat the oven to 400 degrees. Place the butter and flour together in a small bowl and work to a smooth dough by hand. Boil the milk and while hot add the flour and butter mixture, stirring constantly to prevent any lumps from forming. To the thickened milk add the cheese and stir until all of the cheese has melted. Add each egg yolk individually and stir it in thoroughly before adding the next. Beat the egg whites in a separate bowl until stiff. Gently fold the egg whites into the milk mixture. Add salt and pepper according to your taste and pour the mixture into a six-inch soufflé dish which has been greased and dusted with flour. Bake at 400 degrees for about twenty minutes or until golden brown. Serve immediately. Makes four servings.

Cheddar Soufflé

2 eggs	*5 ounces milk*
¼ cup bread crumbs	*½ teaspoon mustard*
4 ounces Cheddar cheese,	*½ teaspoon salt*
grated	*⅛ teaspoon cayenne*

Preheat the oven to 400 degrees. Beat the eggs slightly and add the bread crumbs and the cheese. Boil the milk and add the egg mixture to the milk, stirring until the mixture is smooth and the cheese is melted. Add the seasonings and pour into a greased baking dish. Bake at 400 degrees for about twenty minutes or until the soufflé is set. Makes four servings.

Bacon and Cheese Soufflé

2 strips bacon	*1 cup light cream*
1 pound Swiss cheese, grated	*1 egg*

Preheat the oven to 350 degrees. Fry the bacon until crisp. Crumble the bacon into a mixing bowl and stir in the grated cheese. Add the cream and blend well. Beat the egg and stir into the cheese mixture. Grease four, eight-ounce soufflé dishes and divide the mixture equally among them. Bake the soufflés for fifteen minutes or until set. Serve hot. Makes four servings.

Tomato Soufflé

2 tablespoons butter	*½ teaspoon salt*
2 tablespoons flour	*Dash of pepper*
½ cup milk	*1½ tablespoons melted butter*
1 cup tomato pulp	*½ cup macaroni, cooked*
⅔ cup grated Cheddar	*3 egg yolks*
cheese	*3 egg whites*

Preheat the oven to 350 degrees. Melt the butter and add the flour, stirring until well blended. Gradually add the milk and tomato, stirring constantly. Bring the mixture to the boiling point and simmer for two minutes. Add the cheese, salt, and pepper and stir until the cheese has melted. Add the melted butter to the cooked and drained macaroni and stir in until blended. Add the macaroni to the tomato mixture. Beat the egg yolks until they are thick and lemon colored. Add the yolks to the tomato mixture and blend thoroughly. Beat the egg whites until they are stiff. Slowly and carefully fold the egg whites into the tomato mixture. Butter a deep baking dish and pour the tomato mixture into it. Bake at 350 degrees for about twenty minutes or until the mixture is firm and set. Serve hot. Makes four servings.

Basic Cheese Fondue

7 ounces dry white wine	*3 ounces Kirsch*
1 pound Swiss cheese,	*Pepper*
shredded	*Nutmeg to taste*
1 teaspoon cornstarch	*French bread*

Heat the wine in a fondue pot just to the boiling point. When the wine is just boiling, add the cheese slowly, allowing each portion to melt before adding the next. Stir the mixture constantly to a smooth consistency. Mix the cornstarch with the Kirsch until it is smooth. Stir the Kirsch mixture into the cheese and add the seasonings. Place the pot over a small alcohol flame to keep hot and serve immediately with chunks of French bread and long forks suitable for dipping into the cheese mixture. Makes about three servings.

For a more tangy fondue, replace one half of the Swiss cheese with sharp Cheddar cheese.

Cheese Fondue with Garlic

2 pounds Swiss cheese,
  grated
2 cups dry white wine
1 clove garlic

4 teaspoons cornstarch
5 tablespoons Kirsch
French bread

Cut the cheese into one-half-inch cubes and place them into a salad bowl. Pour the white wine over the cheese and let it soak for about thirty minutes. Pour the white wine from the cheese into a fondue pot and set the pot over a very low heat. Pierce the clove of garlic with a stainless steel fork and use this for stirring the wine while it is heating. Heat the wine just to the boiling point. When the wine just begins to boil, remove the garlic and slowly add the cheese. Stir the wine mixture constantly until the cheese has melted. Stir the cornstarch and Kirsch into the cheese mixture. Use more or less cornstarch depending on how thick the final fondue should be. When the mixture is thoroughly blended and smooth, remove from the heat and place over an alcohol flame to keep hot. Dip chunks of French bread into the fondue using long forks. Makes four or five servings.

Tomato Fondue

8 ounces sharp Cheddar
  cheese, diced
2 ounces blue cheese,
  crumbled
1 teaspoon Worcestershire
  sauce

½ can condensed tomato
  soup
2 tablespoons Kirsch
French bread

Combine the first four ingredients in a fondue pot. Heat gently until the cheeses have melted and the mixture is smooth. Stir in the Kirsch. Remove the pot from the heat and place over an alcohol flame to keep hot. Serve with toasted chunks of French bread. Dip the bread into the cheese mixture using long forks. Makes about one cup of fondue.

Stilton Fondue

This is not the dipping kind of fondue but is the old-style fondue, which is more like a soufflé than a fondue.

¾ cup butter	*8 ounces Stilton cheese,*
2 cups flour	*diced*
5 cups warm milk	*Salt and pepper*
8 egg yolks	*8 egg whites, stiffly beaten*
12 ounces Parmesan cheese,	
grated	

Preheat the oven to 350 degrees. Blend the butter and flour in a large saucepan over a low heat. When the butter is completely melted and well blended with the flour, add the warm milk slowly, stirring constantly. Beat the egg yolks slightly and stir them into the milk mixture. Add the cheeses and stir until the cheese has all melted. Add generous amounts of salt and pepper and blend well. Gently fold in the stiff egg whites. Place eighteen paper baking cups into a muffin tin and divide the cheese mixture among them. Bake for twenty minutes at 350 degrees or until they are nicely browned and set. Serve very hot with the paper peeled off of the sides. Makes eighteen servings.

Neapolitan Pizza

This is not an American pizza but rather a Continental hot lunch.

½ loaf frozen bread dough
10 anchovies
10 ripe olives
4 ounces mozzarella cheese,
shredded
1 clove garlic, chopped

1 pound tomatoes
1 tablespoon chopped
onions
1 teaspoon basil
1 tablespoon olive oil
Salt and pepper to taste

Preheat the oven to 450 degrees. Thaw the bread dough and let it rise. When it has doubled its volume, flatten out the dough and spread it over a well-greased baking sheet. Break up the anchovies and spread them over the dough. Slice the olives and distribute them over the dough. Shred the cheese and mix in the garlic. Spread this mixture over the anchovies and olives. Skin the tomatoes and chop them into large chunks. Sauté the tomatoes, onions, and basil in the oil until slightly done. Season lightly. Pour off the excess liquid and spread the mixture over the cheese. Bake at 450 degrees for about twenty minutes. Makes four servings.

DESSERTS

Ricotta Pie

Pastry Crust (see below)
30 ounces ricotta cheese
1⅓ cups sugar
1 tablespoon flour
4 eggs, slightly beaten
1 teaspoon vanilla

3 tablespoons semisweet
chocolate, coarsely
chopped
3 tablespoons candied
orange peel, chopped
3 tablespoons candied
cherries, chopped

Preheat the oven to 350 degrees. Roll out half of the pastry crust dough to a twelve-inch circle. Fit the crust into a nine-inch pie plate and trim off the edges. Combine the cheese, sugar, and flour in a mixing bowl. Use an electric mixer to beat the ingredients into a smooth mixture. Remove two tablespoons of egg and set them aside. Add the remaining egg and the vanilla to the cheese mixture and beat until light and fluffy. Stir in the chocolate, orange peel, and cherries and blend well.

Spoon the cheese mixture into the prepared pie crust. Roll out the remaining crust into a rectangle and cut it into strips. Weave the strips across the pie to form a lattice cover. Trim off the excess crust. Brush the crust with the reserved egg mixed with one tablespoon of water. Bake at 350 degrees for one hour or until the crust is brown and the filling is firm. Makes eight servings.

Pastry Crust

2 cups sifted flour   2 egg yolks, slightly beaten
½ cup sugar   1 teaspoon vanilla
¾ cup butter

Mix the flour and sugar together in a medium-size bowl. Add the butter and cut into the flour with a pastry blender to form a crumbly mixture. Add the egg yolks and vanilla and mix them in with a fork until the dough holds itself together and does not stick to the sides of the bowl. Chill before using. Makes enough for a nine-inch double crust.

The Lower Calorie Cheesecake

No cheesecake is a dieter's dish but this one comes a little closer.

1 tablespoon butter
½ cup graham cracker
  crumbs
24 ounces fresh Neufchâtel
  cheese
⅔ cup sugar
1½ tablespoons flour

¾ teaspoon grated orange
  rind
1 teaspoon vanilla
3 eggs
1 egg yolk
2 tablespoons skim milk

Preheat the oven to 250 degrees. Butter the sides and bottom of an eight-inch spring-form pan. Sprinkle the graham cracker crumbs over the buttered areas and press into place. Chill the shell in the refrigerator for one hour.

Place the remaining ingredients into an electric blender. Blend at high speed for two minutes or until the mixture is the consistency of heavy cream. Pour the mixture into the lined pan. Bake at 250 degrees for seventy minutes. Allow the cake to cool in the oven with the door open. Remove from the oven when cool and chill for at least four hours before serving. Makes twelve servings.

Italian Pudding

10 ounces ricotta cheese
Scant ½ cup sugar
3 ounces almonds, chopped
¼ teaspoon almond extract

5 egg whites
¼ teaspoon grated lemon
  peel
¼ cup bread crumbs

Preheat the oven to 350 degrees. Force the ricotta through a sieve and into a bowl. Add the sugar, almonds, and almond extract to the cheese and blend well. Beat the egg whites until they peak and add them to the cheese mixture. Stir in the lemon peel. Pour the mixture into a buttered mold. Sprinkle the bread crumbs over the top and bake for thirty minutes at 350 degrees. Makes six servings.

Russian Pudding

8 ounces of egg noodles	*⅛ teaspoon salt*
1 egg	*1 tablespoon cultured cream*
4 ounces cream cheese	*1 tablespoon butter*
1 tablespoon sugar	*1 tablespoon bread crumbs*

Preheat the oven to 350 degrees. Cook the noodles in salted water until they are soft; drain off the water. Beat the egg slightly and add to the noodles. Blend in the cheese, sugar and salt. Work the mixture until well blended. Butter a pie plate generously and spoon the cheese mixture into it. Sprinkle on the bread crumbs and bake at 350 degrees for about twenty minutes. Makes four servings.

Creamed Coffee Cheesecake

¾ cup sugar	*1 teaspoon vanilla*
2 tablespoons unflavored	*2 egg whites*
gelatin	*¼ cup sugar*
¼ teaspoon salt	*1 cup heavy cream*
2 egg yolks, beaten	*½ cup graham cracker*
1 cup milk	*crumbs*
2 tablespoons instant coffee	*1 tablespoon sugar*
24 ounces large curd	*2 tablespoons melted*
cottage cheese, creamed	*butter*

Blend the sugar, gelatin, and salt together and add the eggs and milk. Cook over a low heat, stirring constantly, until the gelatin has dissolved. Blend in the instant coffee and cool the mixture. Force the cottage cheese through a sieve and add the vanilla. Add the cheese mixture to the egg mixture and blend well. Chill the mixture until it begins to hold its own shape when spooned. Beat the egg whites; slowly add the sugar to the egg whites and continue beating until stiff peaks can be formed. Fold the egg whites into the cheese mixture. Whip the heavy cream and fold it into the cheese mixture. Pour the mixture into a nine-inch spring-form pan. Combine the remaining ingredients and blend them with a fork until uniform. Sprinkle the crumb mixture over the cake. Chill for at least four hours before serving. Makes twelve servings.

Strawberry Cheesecake Tarts

¼ cup sugar
¼ cup butter, melted
1½ cups graham cracker
   crumbs
11 ounces cream cheese
½ cup sugar

1 egg
2¼ cups frozen strawberries,
   drained
1 tablespoon sugar
½ cup cultured cream

Preheat the oven to 375 degrees. Line a twelve-hole muffin pan with paper liners. In a separate bowl combine one-fourth cup sugar and butter with the cracker crumbs. Blend thoroughly with a fork and remove two tablespoons for use later. Press the remaining crumbs on the bottoms and sides of the paper cups. Place the crumb shells into the refrigerator to chill. Beat the cream cheese until it is smooth and add one-half cup of sugar a little at a time; add the egg and beat until well blended. Stir in the strawberries. Remove the shells from the refrigerator and spoon the cheese mixture into each shell. Bake for twenty minutes at 375 degrees. While the tarts are baking, mix the remaining sugar with the cultured cream. When the tarts are done remove them from the oven and spoon some of the cultured cream mixture onto each tart.

Sprinkle a little of the reserved crumb mixture over the cultured cream and allow the tarts to cool. Chill and serve cold. Makes twelve tarts.

The last recipe I will give you is a truly rare one. It seems that there is very little use for whey. Mixing it with ground meal and feeding it to hogs is just about its only use. Back in the olden days it was recommended for certain types of obscure illnesses but in these modern times it is not used at all. Whey is dried and used as a commercial food additive but never as a liquid ingredient in home recipes. Now it is with doubtful pleasure that I present to you a genuine recipe for the use of whey. I must confess that I have not tried this recipe but only because I have a preconceived notion that I would not like the stuff anyway.

Whey Lemonade

1 quart sour whey   *Dash of nutmeg or*
2 tablespoons sugar   *cinnamon*
Juice of 2 lemons

Mix all of the above ingredients, chill, and serve over ice. Makes about four servings. (Circa 1896)

Appendix 1

CHEESE-MAKING STARTER
CULTURES, HOW TO GROW
THEM AND WHERE TO GET
THEM

Buttermilk and yogurt can serve as adequate starters for
cheese making but, as I said in Chapter 4, if you wish
reliable and predictable results it is best to grow your own
culture. A freshly made culture will be very active and will
produce acid at the proper rate as soon as it is added to the
milk. Buttermilk and yogurt may, unfortunately, spend days
or even weeks in storage before you buy them for use. The
activity of the organisms are continually declining as they are
stored.

There are two ways to prepare suitable cultures for cheese
making. The first is to prepare a culture from a commercial
end product such as buttermilk or yogurt and the second is
to use commercial freeze-dried culture powders. The second

method is somewhat more expensive but is much more reliable. Both methods can produce suitable cultures for home cheese making, however.

Lactic culture can be made from buttermilk. Instead of adding the buttermilk to the milk as a starter for cheese making, the buttermilk is added to milk and allowed to develop into a mother culture. This mother culture in turn is used to make lactic culture which is used as the starter in cheese making. Lactic culture powder can be substituted for buttermilk and a starter culture prepared in the same way.

To prepare a lactic starter you will need a canning kettle with a rack, two pint-size Mason jars with lids and and rings, fresh *cultured* buttermilk or freeze-dried lactic culture, and a quart of fresh skim milk.

Place enough water in the kettle to cover the jars and begin heating the water. Place the jars, lids, rings, a tablespoon measure, and a stirring spoon into the water. Bring the water to a full boil and boil the utensils for five minutes to sterilize them.

Remove the jars from the hot water with a pair of tongs and allow them to cool. Fill each jar three-quarters full of skim milk. Use the tongs to get a lid and ring from the hot water and place them on the jar. The rings should be loose on the jar so that air can escape from under the lid.

Heat treat the milk by placing the jars of milk into the kettle and filling the kettle with water so that the level of the water is just above the level of the milk in the jars. Cover the kettle and heat the water to 200 degrees. Hold the water at 200 degrees for one hour. After one hour remove each jar from the water and tighten the ring to seal the lid.

Place one jar in the refrigerator for future use and allow the other to cool to 70 degrees. This jar will be used to receive the primary inoculation of lactic organisms.

When the milk has cooled to 70 degrees open the jar. Use

the sterilized measure and add one tablespoon of buttermilk or one gram of lactic culture to the milk. Stir the milk with a sterile spoon for about one minute and then remove the spoon and reseal the jar.

Let the milk stand undisturbed at 70 degrees for sixteen hours. The milk should have developed into a smooth, jelly-like curd. If it has not curdled after sixteen hours let it stand for another eight hours. If the milk has not curdled it is probably because the buttermilk was no longer active. The only thing you can do in this case is to get a new supply of buttermilk and start over with the remaining jar of milk.

Assuming that all has gone well and your milk has coagulated into a smooth curd, you can proceed with the propagation of a starter culture. Heat the jar of milk from the refrigerator to 70 degrees. Open the jar and add one teaspoon of culture from the first jar to the milk in the second jar. Be sure to use sterilized spoons to measure and stir the milk. Reseal the second jar and allow it to stand at 70 degrees for sixteen hours or until it has curdled. The contents of the first jar should be discarded since the activity of these organisms is probably questionable for cheese making.

When the milk in the second jar has curdled refrigerate it immediately. The contents of this jar can now be used as lactic starter for about four days if it is kept refrigerated. After four days use the remaining contents of the second jar to inoculate a third jar of heat-treated milk following the same procedure as before. As each new jar is started the remainder of the previous jar should be discarded. After two months, discard all of the existing cultures and begin the process again using a fresh supply of buttermilk or lactic culture powder.

If at any time during these two months the starters fail to coagulate or your cheese turns out weak-bodied and runny, discard all of the existing cultures, sterilize all of the equipment, and begin again. Failure to coagulate indicates an inactive or contaminated starter and keeping it will only add to your problems.

The second culture commonly used in cheese making is a combination of *Streptococcus thermophilus* and *Lactobacillus bulgaricus*. These organisms are present in yogurt and are much easier to maintain than lactic cultures because they remain active for considerably more time. The disadvantage in using yogurt is that the ratio of one organism to the other may not be the desired one to one ratio. The easiest way to overcome this disadvantage is to buy a freeze-dried yogurt culture available at any health food store or mail-order health food distributor. Starting with a freeze-dried culture assures a more even ratio between the two organisms.

To prepare a combination culture for cheese making use the following procedure rather than those supplied with the culture.

Heat one pint of skim milk or homogenized whole milk, in a water bath, to 195 degrees. Hold the milk at 195 degrees for one hour then cool it to 104 degrees. When the milk has cooled, add the freeze-dried culture and stir it vigorously for one minute. If you do not wish to use a freeze-dried culture, add one teaspoon of fresh yogurt to the milk.

Hold the milk at 104 degrees for about eight hours or until the milk has coagulated. The first coagulation normally requires about eight hours and succeeding coagulations require about three to four hours.

When the milk has coagulated, place it in the refrigerator and store the culture at 40 degrees. Combination cultures will remain active for about ten days at 40 degrees. After ten days, heat treat a fresh supply of milk and use the existing culture to inoculate the milk. Instead of discarding the old culture, however, try eating it. I think you will find it a superior yogurt compared to the commercially available products.

Combination cultures can be used to inoculate fresh supplies of milk for two months. After two months a new freeze-dried culture should be used to inoculate the milk.

Now, you ask, where do I get these cultures? There are several companies from which cultures and other cheese-making supplies can be obtained. These companies are actually laboratories set up to grow specific cultures for the dairy industry. Writing to them will usually bring you a wealth of technical information and a long list of available cultures and molds for cheese making. In addition, these laboratories can supply you with rennet and cheese coloring. The following is a partial list of commercial culture suppliers.

Dairy Laboratories
2300 Locust Street
Philadelphia, Pa. 19103

Chr. Hansen's Laboratory
9015 West Maple Street
Milwaukee, Wisc. 53214

Marshall Dairy Laboratory
14 Proudfit Street
Madison, Wisc. 53703

New Jersey Dairy Laboratories
P. O. Box 748
New Brunswick, N.J. 08903

Of these listed I have dealt with only Chr. Hansen's Laboratory. Rennet and color tablets for eight-gallon batches of milk can be purchased from them by individuals. They can also supply two-gram vials of freeze-dried cultures for lactic starters, combination starters, and several other special cultures including *Propionibacterium shermanii*.

In addition to these laboratories there is a retail and mail-order store on the East Coast which specializes in cheese-making supplies. Homecrafts, 111 Stratford Center, Winston-Salem, N.C. 27104 will send you a free catalogue of just about anything you might need to make cheese.

Another source not to be overlooked are the many wine-making supply stores springing up all over the country. Many of these stores have broadened their lines to include all sorts of food craft equipment including cheese-making equipment.

Appendix 2

THE CURING CHAMBER

Many of the cheeses you will make require long curing times at a very high humidity and low temperature. Other cheeses require, is addition, contact with certain mold growths. Both of these conditions can be more easily met if you have some kind of a curing room. Since you will probably be making very small quantities of cheese the room need not be very large. And since this room can be small, it may as well be small enough to fit into a refrigerator so that it can be kept cool enough for curing cheese.

The curing room I have in mind is a wooden chamber small enough to fit in the refrigerator. It can be constructed from plywood so that any person handy with tools and wood can build it. The dimensions of the chamber are entirely up to the builder and dependent on the size of the rack available.

For instance, if you have a spare oven rack which is twelve by fourteen inches, the inside of the chamber should be about one quarter inch larger than the rack. Let's continue with this example and construct a curing chamber based on a twelve- by fourteen-inch rack. If you have a different size rack, adjust the dimensions to fit your rack.

Construct the chamber from three-eighths inch, exterior grade plywood. You will need the following materials:

sides, 2 pieces, 12¼"×18"×⅜" exterior plywood,
back, 1 piece, 15"×18"×⅜" exterior plywood,
front, 1 piece, 16"×18¾"×⅜" exterior plywood,
top and bottom, 2 pieces, 12⅝"×15"×⅜" exterior plywood,
2 pieces, 12" long of ¾" quarter-round molding,
6   ¼"×2" long "J" bolts,
6   ¼" wing nuts,
16   1¼" cork stoppers,
waterproof glue, spray enamel, nails, washers, a dial-type hygrometer, and a dial-type thermometer.

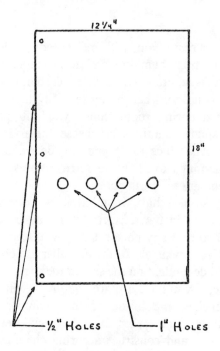

Figure 10. The side of the curing chamber.

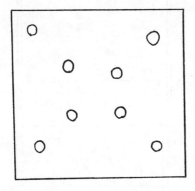

Figure 11. The top of the curing chamber.

Begin with the side pieces. Drill three one-half-inch holes along one of the long edges, see Figure 10. Drill the holes about one and three-eighths inches in from the edge and equally spaced along the edge. Then drill four one-inch holes about seven inches up from the bottom edge. Both side panels should be identical up to this point.

Lay the side panels aside and find the panel which will serve as a top. Drill eight one-inch holes through the top panel. The location of the holes is not important but they should be evenly distributed, see Figure 11.

Glue and nail the back to the two side panels as shown in Figure 12. Use liberal amounts of glue to be sure the joints are sealed. Clamp the panels in place and let the glue dry overnight. Be certain that the three small holes in the side panels are mounted away from the back.

When the glue has dried, remove the clamps and glue and nail the top and bottom panels in place.

Mount the thermometer and hygrometer in one of the side panels. The instrument which I had was a very inexpensive, plastic weather station which had a dial hygrometer and a

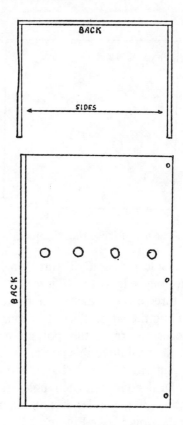

Figure 12. The assembly of the sides and the back.

straight thermometer in one box. Cut a hole in the center of one of the side panels which is about one quarter inch *smaller* than the face of the instrument to be mounted. Place a heavy bead of silicon bathtub caulking around the instrument and press it in place over the hole, see Figure 14. Place a heavy weight on the instrument to hold it down and let the caulking dry overnight. Mount both instruments in the same way if you have a separate thermometer and hygrometer.

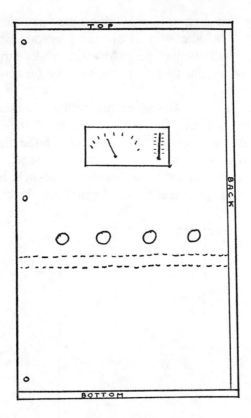

Figure 13. The assembled chamber showing the location of the hygrometer.

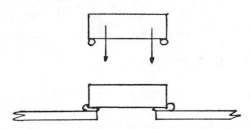

Figure 14. Mounting the instrument over the hole.

Glue the two quarter-round strips onto the sides on the inside of the chamber just *below* the four one-inch holes. These strips will support the wire rack while curing your cheese, so be certain that they are securely fastened to the sides.

Stand the front panel against the curing chamber. There will be a one-half-inch flange on each side of the chamber. Mark the front flange with the location of the three one-half-inch holes along the edge of the side panel. Remove the front panel and drill six five-sixteenths-inch mounting holes into the flange area of the front panel, see Figure 15.

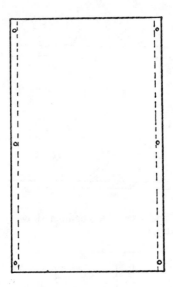

Figure 15. The front panel.

The front panel is secured to the cabinet by hooking the "J" bolts into the holes in the side panels and then passing the shank of the bolt through the front panel. Place a washer and wing nut on the bolt and draw the front down against the sides, see Figure 16.

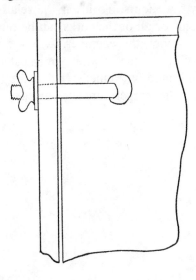

Figure 16. Detail of securing the front panel.

When the assembly of the chamber is complete, paint the entire cabinet, inside and outside, with two coats of spray enamel. Since the appearance is not important do not worry about a drippy paint job or the rough finish but be sure the wood is well covered with paint.

To use the curing chamber place the wire rack on the wooden strips. Place a bowl filled with water under the rack and secure the front panel. Plug all of the holes with corks and stand the curing chamber in the refrigerator. Check the relative humidity after twenty-four hours. The evaporating water should have raised the relative humidity to about 90 per cent. If it is not that high you may need to add some wicks to the bowl. Cut several strips of terry cloth and place them in the water in the bowl and hang them over the edge. Seal the cabinet and check the relative humidity again after another twenty-four hours. To lower the relative humidity in the chamber some or all of the corks can be removed to allow air movement through the chamber. A few weeks of experimenting will tell you exactly what you must do to obtain a specific relative humidity. Remember that the relative humidity will change if the temperature is changed.

INDEX